What Now?

Finding Freedom from the Hardships of Life

ASHLEY AKERS

ISBN: 978-1-7337415-0-7 (Paperback)
ISBN: 978-1-7337415-1-4 (eBook)
Library of Congress Control Number: 2019901962

Front cover picture by Don Burke.
Book design by Ashley Akers.

Published by Ashley Akers, Potosi, Missouri 63664
ashley@whatnowdevo.com

www.whatnowdevo.com

Table of Contents

About the Author

ASHLEY AKERS

My name is Ashley. In 2016, God began prompting me to quit my corporate job and work fulltime in ministry. What now?! As scary as it could have been, I completely relied on the Lord, and with the support of my wonderful husband, Scott, we stepped out in faith. This step marked the season that was a turning point in my life—releasing complete control to the Lord.

The journey I have been on ever since has given me clarity and freedom I could not have imagined. Living life totally dependent on God and experiencing more of who He is ignites passion and days driven by purpose. Currently, I am serving at First Baptist Church in Potosi, MO as a Sunday school teacher, leader of a marriage ministry program, musician and website designer. I am a co-founder of SHINE the Conference and round-the-clock volunteer at Life in Progress Ministries; a ministry dedicated to breaking down barriers to belief and helping people learn, love and live out the Christian faith. I also aid Nonprofits in design. Although I am a licensed Realtor and have a bachelor's degree in accountancy, ministry and sharing the gospel of Jesus are my passion.

Scott and I have been married since June 2002 and have two amazing children. We reside in small-town Potosi, MO.

You can find more information at www.whatnowdevo.com.

Acknowledgements

To my Lord and Savior Jesus Christ for dying on the cross for my sin. Without Him, I would not have been able to experience FREEDOM from my hardships.

To my amazing husband, Scott, for always being by my side. You have always supported me in whatever God has called me to do and always been there to help me with whatever I needed. Your encouraging words to keep going are what helped me to finish.

To my wonderful children, Tyler and Mikella, for understanding and giving me time and space to write.

To my mom, Sheila, for your strength and support. You are the strongest woman I know!

To Jaclyn, Debbie, Don and Pam for helping me through the writing process. I couldn't have done this without you!

Introduction

Life. Is. Hard.

Until I was married at the age of 18, I lived in a physically and mentally abusive home. I lived through really hard things during my childhood and spent many nights crying myself to sleep. The lack of peace in my home, coupled with the witnessing of abuse to my mother deeply affected me—even after I left.

I went to church all my life, but I didn't truly understand and accept Jesus until I was 21 years old. While time did heal to an extent, I was never *fully* healed until I gave all my hurts to the Lord 14 years after I moved out of my childhood home.

The Lord put it on my heart to write this book while teaching at a local pregnancy resource center. Many women walking through those doors were hurting for various reasons, and you may be too. While Jesus never promised that we would be without trouble, He did promise that He would be with us through everything. He has proven this to me over and over again, even through some of my toughest times. He will prove Himself to you, too.

My prayer is that you will give all your struggles and hurts to the Lord, allowing Him to fight your battles for you, and in return you will gain the FREEDOM that is only found in Him.

Through this easy to read topical devotional, you will see my personal struggle, read what scripture says about it, ask yourself questions and apply what you learn to help you overcome. These lessons can be done individually, with a friend or in a small group setting.

We are surrounded by so many lies. It is time to start fighting with the truth.

Abortion

A close friend, who wishes to remain anonymous speaks of her abortion. This is her story.

"At the young age of 17, I was raped at a party. Six months after losing my innocence, I began to date a cute boy.

On our first official date he began pressuring me to go all the way, but I was not ready. My traumatic situation was still fresh in my mind and he wouldn't accept no for an answer, even after my repeatedly telling him no. I buried my emotions as I began to be raped again. I became pregnant after that one and only time. When I told him, he immediately denied it and said *it wasn't his* because I wasn't pure. Fear of rejection from my parents and boyfriend quickly set in. Then came the quiet whisper of the enemy telling me: "Just get rid of it and go on with your life—it's no big deal," "Nobody will ever know you did this," "You are too young for a baby," and "Having a baby will ruin your life."

I began trusting the lies, the medical field, my parents and the boy that rejected me. I thought having an abortion was my only way out and that the choice was made for me. I was being told that the baby wasn't a life until the heartbeat developed, but there was a spirit within me giving me an uncomfortable "This is not right!" feeling. But the spirit of DO IT took over, and quickly. Before I knew it, my parents rushed me to the clinic and paid the $250 fee.

Afterwards, I didn't have a sense of relief that the lies promised me. I still experienced the boy's rejection. Then, the enemy started whispering different phrases such as: "I can't believe you did that," "That was a life and now it's gone," and "God won't forgive you for this." The enemy who talked us into it, shamed me for 33 years and made me experience guilt and silence—nobody could know my secret. This led to hiding, pretending, self-medicating and self-coping."

John 10:10 says,

The thief comes only to steal and kill and destroy. I came that they may have life and have it abundantly.

The "thief" is Satan, our enemy. He will seize every opportunity to ruin lives, just like he tried to do with my friend. The choice to abort was made from a place of fear, and from that fear came 33 years of shame. Fear and confusion are not of God, but of the enemy. Jesus came to die on a cross for our sins so that we "may have life and have it abundantly." You can be free of the shame caused by abortion by confessing your sin to God.

1 John 1:9 says,

If we confess our sins, he is faithful and just to forgive us our sins and to cleanse us from all unrighteousness.

When you humbly ask for forgiveness, you are forgiven. End of story. You are cleansed, and God will never bring it up again. Once my friend confessed and experienced healing through Bible studies, she said, "The FREEDOM of God exceeds the guilt of sin. I am forgiven by my Creator GOD who restores what the enemy had eaten for 33 years." There is HOPE and you or someone you know can experience freedom too!

1. Have you ever experienced an abortion? Describe your experience.

2. Have you experienced God's healing?

Abuse

Abuse. A 5-letter word that makes us cringe every time we hear it. Abuse can be physical, sexual or emotional and leaves you feeling completely helpless to ever recover. You feel bound by a chain and every hurtful thing that is said or done adds yet another link to that chain that seems to grow as long as the sea is wide. You feel there is nowhere to go and no way for the chain to be broken; that you have lost your battle—and maybe even yourself.

If abuse hovers over your life, how might you be reacting? Maybe you grab some paint and try to make your chain look different or prettier, hoping nobody will figure out what your reality is. Or maybe you hide behind a fake persona, but fear that somebody will discover your double life. You worry. What if they find out? Will people look down on me or still like me? Am I worthy enough of help or am I a lost cause? Will I be the talk of the town? Your list of questions runs through your mind and goes on and on. The suffering seems unbearable at times.

How do I know? These thoughts were mine. I once was bound by abusive chains, and I lived that double life as a child/teenager. I wanted people to think that I had the perfect family, but our reality was far from it. Walking on eggshells every.single.day. hurts. The emotional abuse I endured and witnessing the physical abuse of my mother left me grasping for hope and asking "why?"

Did you know that Jesus himself was abused? In Matthew 26:67-68 it says,

> Then they spit in his face and struck him. And some slapped him, saying, "Prophesy to us, you Christ! Who is it that struck you?"

Jesus was publicly humiliated by being spit on, struck and even mocked. The abuse He endured only got exceedingly worse when He was crucified. He did nothing wrong to deserve it. He knows and understands your pain and your struggles. He wants you to know that there IS hope. And that hope is found in Him. He is the only one who can break those chains Satan put on us, removing them link-by-link. Jesus says in Matthew 11:28-30,

> Come to me, all who labor and are heavy laden, and I will give you rest. Take my yoke upon you, and learn from me, for I am gentle and lowly in heart, and you will find rest for your souls. For my yoke is easy, and my burden is light.

Being abused can be a lifelong burden if you choose not to surrender your life to the One and Only Healer, Jesus Christ. He wants a relationship with you and He can break the chains once and for all. How was I able to break free from my chains? First, I surrendered my life to Christ. I realized that I cannot do anything apart from Him. Secondly, I earnestly sought God by reading my Bible and praying. Lastly, I opened up about my past to someone I trusted and I confronted my pain.

1. Have you ever been a victim of any type of abuse in your life? What were/are the circumstances?

2. How have you worked through it?

3. Are you ready to release your burdens and allow Jesus to cut the chains by taking the steps described in the last paragraph?

Accountability

In today's world, accountability seems to be a word we would like scratched from our dictionary. Nothing is our fault and the blame game is like a merry-go-round that makes us dizzy with confusion. When I got in trouble as a child, my mom would attempt to discipline me for what I did wrong. Lucky for me, I figured out that if I ran around her in a circle she couldn't keep up with me and she would eventually wear out and give up. One significant lesson came from this: Because I was rarely held accountable for my actions I figured I could just "run" from my bad choices and never have to pay the penalties.

I may have been able to execute great escapes from my mother when I was a child, but I've discovered over time that I can't exactly get away with running from God. He holds us accountable for our beliefs, for our words and for our actions. Jesus said in John 3:18,

> Whoever believes in Him [Jesus] is not condemned, but whoever does not believe is condemned already, because he has not believed in the name of the only Son of God.

Wow, let that one sink in. Who is condemned? Whoever does not believe in Jesus! After you die you will appear before God and be judged based upon whether or not you believed in Christ. If you don't believe, your punishment will be eternal. God doesn't wear out and let us go punishment-free. God follows through on His word. He cannot lie. Whether you are ready or not, you will have to face your fate. Your destiny can be heaven if you choose to accept Christ. Simple. Or it will have to be hell if you reject Him.

Scripture also teaches that believers too—while they will go to heaven—still must stand before Jesus and be judged for how they lived. As 2 Corinthians 5:10 says,

> For we must all appear before the judgment seat of Christ, so that each one may receive what is due for what he has done in the body, whether good or evil.

Matthew 12:36 says,

> I tell you, on the day of judgment people will give account for every careless word they speak.

Why does the Bible make it clear that we will be judged for even our careless words? Because our words reveal the truth of our hearts! What ugliness lurks in the deepest places of your heart? Take a moment to think about that. Yes, in Christ we enjoy the free gift of grace; but we must never use His grace as a cover for wrong beliefs, thoughts, words or actions. We will still have to answer to God for how we lived in light of His amazing grace.

Are you ready to be held accountable for your actions whether good or bad?

1. What fears do you have when you think about the day you will die and meet Jesus face to face?

2. How have you been shown grace by God or another person despite your actions?

3. Have you made the choice to believe in Christ and accept Him? If Yes, how can you improve your relationship with Christ? If No, please turn to the topic, "Salvation".

4. Are there any amends you need to make with someone you have treated poorly?

Accusations

Have you ever been accused of something? I have. And I don't think any of us are exempt from it. For me, working in an office dominated by women guaranteed being accused of something! Jealousy flared up, and out the accusations poured like water when a dam breaks. I would feel the rushing tide and throw on my life jacket so I wouldn't drown. I learned that fighting to keep my head above the flood of accusations was much better than drowning in them and feeling defeated.

Here are a few things I did to stay afloat. First, I literally placed scripture on my computer monitor to remind me of God's promises and of who I am in Him. Second, I decided to love those who were making the accusations. Third, I focused on Christ and not what other people thought of me. Finally, I learned to filter the accusations for truth. If I had indeed done wrong, I would repent (change my mind) toward God and He would extend forgiveness and not accusation.

Colossians 1:21-22 NLT says:

> This includes you who were once far away from God. You were his enemies, separated from him by your evil thoughts and actions. Yet now he has reconciled you to himself through the death of Christ in his physical body. As a result, he has brought you into his own presence, and you are holy and blameless as you stand before him without a single fault.

No one is good. No.not.one. We are all born with a sinful nature, which automatically creates distance between God and us. In order to close that gap for good, Jesus Christ—God wrapped in flesh—walked on this earth as a sinless man. He died in your place and mine. He took the punishment for our sin when His blood was shed on a cross so that we could live forever with Him in heaven. When you accept Christ as your personal Lord and Savior and ask Him to forgive your sins, He does; and He chooses to forget them. It is like your sin never happened. Read Colossians 1:22 above again. You can be "…holy and blameless as you stand before him without a single fault." When our confidence is solely in Jesus, it doesn't matter what we have done because He has chosen to wipe our slates clean. Praise God!

Matthew 27:12-14 NLT says:

> But when the leading priests and the elders made their accusations against him, Jesus remained silent. "Don't you hear all these charges they are bringing against you?" Pilate demanded. But Jesus made no response to any of the charges, much to the governor's surprise.

When Jesus was accused, He didn't retaliate or threaten his accusers. He didn't even say a word. The next time you find yourself being accused, consider being like Jesus. Leave it with God and let Him take care of you.

1. Read Matthew 27:12-14 again. How does this scripture speak to you and how can you do better in your own life when being accused?

2. What have you been accused of in your past that you are still holding on to? Is there any truth in the accusation that you need to repent of?

3. Look up the word forgive in the dictionary. What is the definition?

4. Are you ready to forgive the person that accused you and give it to God? Not forgiving others always hurts you more than it does them.

Adoption

B ack in 2012, my life was totally hectic, but joyful. I was working full time, going to college full time to get my bachelor's degree, our son was 9 and on top of that, my husband and I were foster parents to a spunky 7-year-old girl. One day I received a phone call from Division of Family Services saying that there was a two-month-old baby girl needing a home and they asked if the baby could be placed with us. I spoke to my sleep-deprived, night-shift-working husband about it and we agreed to keep her for the weekend to see how the dynamics would work in our already crazy lives.

I remember holding that baby girl for the first time like it was yesterday. A spark or a connection happened that I can't explain. What I knew in that moment was that God had special plans in store for us. After a year of being her foster parents, God gave us the opportunity to adopt her. She is now just as much a part of our family as she would be if she had been born to us, and she even has a new birth certificate with our names as the parents.

Did you know that when you accept Christ, you are adopted into God's family? John 1:12-13 NLT says,

> But to all who believed him and accepted him, he gave the right to become children of God. They are reborn-not with a physical birth resulting from human passion or plan, but a birth that comes from God.

Ephesians 1:4-5 NLT adds,

> Even before he made the world, God loved us and chose us in Christ to be holy and without fault in his eyes. God decided in advance to adopt us into his own family by bringing us to himself through Jesus Christ. This is what he wanted to do, and it gave him great pleasure.

When you accept Christ, a spark or a connection happens that you can't explain either. You are filled with such joy and love that nobody can take away from you. In that moment, you become HIS. You become an heir with Jesus and will inherit all that God's kingdom has! You are reborn spiritually into this new family with God as your father and Jesus as your brother. How cool is that?! When you are physically born, your body is physically alive. When you are reborn spiritually, you become spiritually alive. You will notice that your actions, your attitudes and your choices change.

Never forget that God chose you. You are loved. You are cherished. You are adopted into His family and nothing is better than that.

1. Describe your experience of being adopted into God's family. (If you have not been adopted into God's family, go to the topic "Salvation" for guidance.)

2. What are some similarities between your earthly father and your heavenly father?

3. What are some differences between your earthly father and your heavenly father?

Alcohol

When I was a young teen I would earn a little extra money by babysitting a little boy, who was a toddler at the time. I would watch him on the weekends so his parents could go out on a date. I discovered that usually meant they went out to party and drink with their friends. I hadn't been around alcohol and those who use it, so I didn't understand the effects it could have on a person. But one cold winter night that all changed. The party-goers returned around 11:00 p.m. To my horror, the dad of this little boy came raging through the door, running from one end of the house to the other, snarling and growling and obviously out of control. He was drooling and claiming to see the devil.

Romans 13:13-14 NLT says:

> Because we belong to the day, we must live decent lives for all to see. Don't participate in the darkness of wild parties and drunkenness…. Instead, clothe yourself with the presence of the Lord Jesus Christ. And don't let yourself think about the ways to indulge your evil desires.

"Alcohol" comes from the Arabic root word Al kol, which refers to any drug or substance that takes away the mind or covers it. When a person becomes drunk, they are not in control of their own mind. If you are not in control of your mind, Satan will be glad to control it for you. His mission: kill, steal and destroy! How can you be focused on living as God wants you to? You can't. The Bible clearly says to avoid drunkenness for good reason. Stay away!

Notice also what Galatians 5:16-21NLT says:

> So I say, let the Holy Spirit guide your lives. Then you won't be doing what your sinful nature craves. The sinful nature wants to do evil, which is just the opposite of what the Spirit wants. And the Spirit gives us desires that are the opposite of what the sinful nature desires. These two forces are constantly fighting each other… When you follow the desires of your sinful nature, the results are very clear: sexual immorality, impurity, lustful pleasures… drunkenness, wild parties, and other sins like these.

If you allow the Holy Spirit to guide and empower your life, you will be able to resist the temptations that your sinful flesh desires. The devil is a liar and he will try to convince you that one drink won't hurt. Then he will tempt you with "just one more," then another, then another until you are drunk.

Have you become dependent on alcohol to make you feel happy or likeable? The pleasant effects of alcohol are temporary. The devil wants to hold you and convince you that drinking will make you happy. My friends, the Lord longs for you to discover that happiness and joy are found in Christ, not from a bottle.

1.   What is your purpose for wanting to indulge in alcohol, whether one glass or ten?

2.   Does your desire to drink glorify God?

3.   How has alcohol led you into more sin? (For example: drugs, lust, sexual immorality, anger, fighting, etc.)

Anger

…he didn't listen to *me* and she didn't do it *my* way.

"My name is Ashley Akers. I am a grateful believer in Jesus Christ and I struggle with anger." This is the acknowledgement I shared each week at a recovery meeting at my church. I have struggled with anger all my life. I was even given the nickname Spitfire years ago after I exploded in anger on a poor hotel desk clerk for giving our room away. Did my anger do any good? No. Did I win that fight? No. Was I acting like a fool? Yes. How I wish I could go back to that day and do it all over again. I wish I knew then what I know now. My anger can build very quickly with the ones I love, and this has made me question why I get angry. My reasons usually sounded something like these: I am mad because they said something about me, she hurt me, he didn't listen to me and she didn't do it my way. Do you notice a common denominator? They are all about me! When I am in a selfish frame of mind, I tend to speak more and listen less because I want to be heard. Then when things don't go my way, I become angry. When I'm focused on myself there is no possibility my focus is also on God, where it should be.

James 1:19-20 NLT says:

> *Understand this, my dear brothers and sisters: You must all be quick to listen, slow to speak, and slow to get angry. Human anger does not produce the righteousness God desires.*

And Ephesians 4:26-27 NLT says:

> *And don't sin by letting anger control you. Don't let the sun go down while you are still angry, for anger gives a foothold to the devil.*

Not all anger is bad. But the kind of anger that is sometimes called "the wrath of men" is bad. I would describe this as self-centered anger because it tends to, well, center on you. God does not desire for you to be weighed down with a life marked by your temper! Anger will produce conflict, pride, loneliness and bitterness that can destroy relationships. When we act out of selfish anger in any circumstance, the devil gains breeding ground to work in our lives and in our relationships, just like Ephesians said. Resentment settles into the cracks where cooperation used to preside, gossip starts, which leads to more hurt and even greater anger. Do you see the repetitive pattern uncontrolled anger can cause? Eventually the cracks become great divides and the relationship is severely damaged. You must break that cycle. Don't allow waves of negative emotion to weigh you down or hurt the people around you. Settle arguments quickly with loving words instead. Anger is an emotion that God created us to experience, but what you get mad about and how you deal with anger when it arises determines if it is sinful or not. Your reactions and responses are your choice.

So the question is, how do you get rid of sinful anger? First, you must PRAY! Express to your Lord, Jesus Christ, how desperately you need Him to help. Then, own up to your sinful anger with God and with a spiritually mature person you trust. I challenge you to walk closely with Christ and to continually seek Him through prayer and through His Word, the Bible. The more we see and strive to live by His ways the more we can break away from anger's evil grip and destruction in our lives.

1. What do you find yourself angry about most of the time?

2. What do you find is the root of your anger?

3. What steps do you need to take to help with your sinful anger?

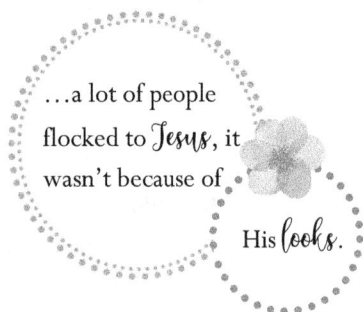

Appearance

L et me ask you a serious question. Have you ever avoided speaking to someone because of their appearance? The answer can be applied in two ways. You may have avoided them because they weren't dressed very well or because they were dressed too nice. Or instead of clothes your reluctance may have been based on their beauty (or lack thereof). Either way, your actions could have been based upon how the person looked.

James 2:2-4 NLT tells us not to judge people based upon appearance and when we do it reveals our true heart.

> *"Suppose someone comes into your meeting dressed in fancy clothes and expensive jewelry, and another comes in who is poor and dressed in dirty clothes. If you give special attention and a good seat to the rich person, but you say to the poor one, "You can stand over there, or else sit on the floor"—well, doesn't this discrimination show that your judgments are guided by evil motives?"*

You know the golden rule, "treat others how you wish to be treated." Easier said than done. Consider this: What do you think Jesus looked like? Tall, dark and handsome? Bright blue eyes with long flowing hair? Maybe he even looked like a man straight out of a magazine? When you try to picture what Jesus looked like, you probably think of Him as attractive and that everybody loved Him for his beauty. Not so. While it's true a lot of people flocked to Jesus, it wasn't because of His looks. In fact, He wasn't even considered attractive at all. Isaiah 53:2-4 NLT describes Him.

> *He [Jesus] had no beauty or majesty to attract us to him, nothing in his appearance that we should desire him…*

Jesus wasn't particularly attractive but was still obviously used by God. So maybe you shouldn't be overly concerned about what you or others look like on the outside? You can become so fixated on the outward appearance that you miss the true beauty within.

Jesus did not want people to follow Him based upon his outward appearance, but by His true inward character. Let the light of Jesus shining through you be your beauty, and do not be overly concerned with your outward appearance.

1. How often do you focus on the outward appearance of a person? Be honest with yourself.

2. Use your Bible or Bible app to read 1 Peter 3:1-6. What do these verses mean?

3. Before reading this devotional how did you mentally picture what Jesus looked like? How is that different now?

Arguments

When I was growing up arguments were a common occurrence in everyday life. Ironically, there was one thing I noticed; there was never a winner. Nothing ever got settled, there were always hurt feelings and it was always somebody else's fault. So, as a child I quickly picked up how to argue. My mother always said that I should be an attorney because I would argue with a fence post. And one thing was certain; I wouldn't stop until I won. For me "picking my battles" meant picking every battle because I was determined to not be beat by anyone. I couldn't and wouldn't accept defeat.

But, to my dismay, the Bible teaches us not to argue and for good reason. Philippians 2:14 NLT says:

Do everything without ... arguing.

And 2 Timothy 2:23 NLT notes,

Again I say, don't get involved in foolish, ignorant arguments that only start fights.

That verse is a hard one for me! Arguing can have serious consequences and can cause others to lose respect for you—respect very hard to regain. We live in an electronic age where voicing your opinion has become easy, way too easy. The boom of social media has taken arguing to an unprecedented level. Hiding behind a computer can give one a sense of confidence. This confidence can be used for good but is often used for bad. Think of a recent time you posted something argumentative or saw somebody else do that kind of thing. Posts range from ranting to trying to prove a person wrong to intentionally demeaning someone else or even trying to expose a person. Posts like that hurt feelings, damage reputations and start fights that are not easily resolved, if ever. It is far better to practice self-discipline when you feel like arguing in a way that is not glorifying to God. This is super hard, especially if you have the "foot-in-mouth syndrome" like I do. I normally remind myself, "Think before you speak, Ashley. Think before you speak." Sometimes I do well and sometimes I fail. If I fall, I get right back up by swallowing my pride, apologizing and moving on while trying to do better.

Not only can arguing negatively affect you, it can negatively affect the church. Constant arguing gives unbelievers a false picture of who Jesus is. Why would anybody want to trust Jesus and be a part of His church if it appears that all Christians do is argue? The greatest commands that Jesus gave us were to love God and to love others. LOVE. Love the one who gossips about you or tries to argue with you. Amazingly, loving others helps you win the war by refusing to engage in the battle.

1. Do you find yourself wanting to argue with others?

2. Why do you normally want to argue?

3. How do you react when others try to argue with you?

We are *constantly* fighting in a spiritual *battle* we may not see, but we certainly *experience*.

Armor

When I hear the word "armor," I immediately think of battle. Armor is used to shield or protect someone or something important. We normally think of this protection in a physical sense, but for the Christian, the Bible teaches us about a spiritual armor, "the armor of God".

We are constantly fighting in a spiritual battle we may not see, but we certainly experience. Every person feels the intensity of the devil and his schemes and must learn to fight against them. Ephesians 6:13-18 NLT explains how:

> *Therefore, put on every piece of God's armor so you will be able to resist the enemy in the time of evil. Then after the battle you will still be standing firm. Stand your ground, putting on the belt of truth and the body armor of God's righteousness. For shoes, put on the peace that comes from the Good News so that you will be fully prepared. In addition to all of these, hold up the shield of faith to stop the fiery arrows of the devil. Put on salvation as your helmet, and take the sword of the Spirit, which is the word of God. Pray in the Spirit at all times and on every occasion. Stay alert and be persistent in your prayers for all believers everywhere.*

You may be asking what exactly this means, and how to "put on" this armor? First, examine the pieces. The second paragraph lists the various pieces of armor for us. Let's consider each one.

Putting on the **belt of truth** means we make it a priority to learn the truths that God gives us in His Word. The **body armor** (which functioned like a bullet-proof vest that protects a police officer from a gunshot) illustrates how righteousness, or living by God's guidelines, protects the Christian. As you make right choices, God is able to protect your heart. His standards provide protection for your thoughts and feelings, including things like emotions, doubt, shame and questions of self-worth. When scripture lists **shoes**, it is saying that understanding the Good News of Jesus, gives us an inner stability that allows us to both, stand firm and to go where He has asked to share Jesus with others.

Shield of faith is basically saying to trust in God—even if you don't see His way working. When you trust God enough to live as He says, you will have protection, a shield, from the ways Satan attacks you. For example, temptations can be like fiery arrows coming at you from any direction. But, when we have faith in and pursue God's plans, He provides a way out so we do not have to fall victim to attacks!

Most importantly, put on your **helmet**, which is salvation. Think for a moment about what a helmet does. It protects your head. In a successful attack, if the head is left unprotected, all is lost. Without the helmet of salvation, Satan will eventually win the battle when you die and you are lost for all eternity. Make sure your salvation is securely in place.

Lastly, take up the **sword of the Spirit**, which is God's word. God's word is truth and is our weapon to fight against the devil's schemes. Read it, memorize it, ponder how it applies to your life and use it to fight. You'll win.

So, how does all of this come together? By praying at all times. You develop warrior strength and secure your armor by talking with God throughout each day and depending on His Spirit. Pray for yourself, for others, for His will and for His help all day long.

1. What kind of temptations are you currently facing?

2. A soldier wears his armor all the time he's on the battlefield, not just occasionally. As a Christian soldier, do you have all your armor on all the time, every day?

Assurance

Assurance is a *confidence*, a *guarantee* and a *freedom* from doubt.

When I was younger, around age 8, I went to a revival service at a local church. As the preacher ended the message, he invited anybody who would like to be "saved" to come to the front. Naturally, I went to the front. I didn't exactly understand, but everybody else was going and I didn't want to be left out. So, I repeated the words of the prayer he suggested, got baptized, and went on with my life as a "faithful church member."

Fast forward to age 21, when I had a serious medical emergency and could have died. Facing the reality of death really scared me and continued to weigh heavily on my mind. God began dealing with me and I felt uneasy in my heart. Six months later, I was at church and my pastor offered this helpful advice: "If you are not sure if you are saved, ask God to convict you of your need for salvation or to give you peace if you are already saved." I knew in those moments that God gave him that message specifically for me. Over the next five days I prayed that prayer and God's conviction was very strong. On Friday night, I prayed—sincerely—asking Jesus into my heart. In that moment, I had a peace that nothing else had ever given me and I knew that if I were to die I *would* go to heaven. I was "saved" and had *assurance* in that moment! Furthermore, because of that decision made in a moment of genuine surrender, nothing has nor ever will be able to separate me from God and His love. Romans 8:35-39 gives me this proof:

> *Can anything ever separate us from Christ's love? Does it mean he no longer loves us if we have trouble or calamity, or are persecuted, or hungry, or destitute, or in danger, or threatened with death? ... No, despite all these things, overwhelming victory is ours through Christ, who loved us. And I am convinced that nothing can ever separate us from God's love. Neither death nor life, neither angels nor demons, neither our fears for today nor our worries about tomorrow—not even the powers of hell can separate us from God's love. No power in the sky above or in the earth below—indeed, nothing in all creation will ever be able to separate us from the love of God that is revealed in Christ Jesus our Lord."*

Jesus said:

> *I tell you the truth, those who listen to my message and believe in God who sent me have eternal life. They will never be condemned for their sins, but they have already passed from death into life.* (John 5:24)

By trusting in Jesus Christ, you can have assurance too. Assurance is a confidence, a guarantee and a freedom from doubt. Assurance will chase away fear and the bondage that comes with it. Jesus wants to turn your fear into a peace that only He can give. He loves you. There is no fear or trouble or person or thing that will ever separate you from His love.

1. Use your Bible or Bible app and read John 10:28. Who can snatch you away from Jesus?

2. Re-read Romans 8:35-39 above. What *cannot* separate you from God's love?

3. What are you fearful of?

Atonement

Atonement. What does that strange looking word even mean? It is described as "satisfaction or payment for a wrong".

You may be sitting there wondering if you have *ever* done anything wrong. If that thought even crosses your mind, let me just kindly say, you are in denial. Of course you have done wrong things. Who hasn't? When it comes to doing and being all that I should, I'm certain I mess up every single day; and regrettably, that won't change tomorrow. There was only one person born perfect, and it wasn't me! Nobody had to teach any of us how to do bad things. Nobody taught my precious little 4-year-old girl to hide chocolate from me and then lie about eating it—despite the evidence all over her face. I didn't teach her to lie, but I do have to teach her to tell the truth, and at times that teaching involves punishment for lying.

Here's the thing; we all sin or do wrong. We generally get that part. But do you realize that there is a price that must be paid for sin? This is where that strange looking word *atonement* comes into the picture. The Bible is made up of two different sections; the Old Testament and the New Testament. In the Old Testament and in the beginning of the New Testament until Jesus' death, people had to *sacrifice* an animal, shedding its' blood, for the atonement (payment) of their sins. And it couldn't be just any animal. They needed to bring a perfect animal, without any kind of blemish. When they sacrificed the animal, God was willing to forgive their sins.

"So, why don't we still have to do that?" you may be wondering. It's because God provided the ULTIMATE sacrifice, His Son Jesus Christ, who forever atoned for our sin and satisfied the requirements of God. Romans 3:23-25 says:

> For everyone has sinned; we all fall short of God's glorious standard. Yet God freely and graciously declares that we are righteous. He did this through Christ Jesus when he freed us from the penalty for our sins. For God presented Jesus as the sacrifice for sin. People are made right with God when they believe that Jesus sacrificed his life, shedding his blood....

Jesus died on a cross, shedding His blood, for both you and me. Now, when we ask Him for forgiveness, our slate is wiped clean of all our sin—even the one you think is too bad or unforgiveable. Jesus paid the price for all sin, and there is not any sin beyond His blood. Atonement becomes a beautiful word when we understand how Jesus lost His life to save ours and because of His love, we give our lives to Him.

1.   Are you holding on to any sins because you think they are too big for Jesus to forgive?

2.   Use your Bible or Bible app to read 1 Peter 3:18. What emotions well up inside of you when you think about Christ suffering and dying for your sins?

Attitude

Have you ever taken a personality test? I have. The color associated with my personality type is RED. You know, the person who likes to control, can be prideful, gets angry quickly, is easily irritated, intimidating; shall I go on? Yes, I am *that* kind of person. By nature, I am an in-your-face, just-let-me-do-it, get-out-of-the-way, my-way-is-better, don't-think-before-I-speak type person. And before I know it, I am throwing around my opinion like nobody's business, because, naturally, I think that I am right, and the other person is wrong.

In short, I can have an attitude.

But, just because these are natural characteristics of my personality, I can't excuse a bad attitude or bad behavior. That was the old me. I have lived and learned — and sometimes learned the hard way. The Holy Spirit has His work cut out for Him, but I'm grateful He always course corrects me when I am out-of-line. He even requires me to go back to whomever I've hurt and apologize. What? Apologize? Saying, "I'm sorry" shows others that I was wrong, and for a RED person, that is worse than pulling teeth! Why is it so painful? Because it requires humility and I am forced to deal with my pride.

Philippians 2:5 NLT says,

> *"You must have the same attitude that Christ Jesus had."*

What kind of attitude did Jesus have? First of all, He was humble. Jesus made himself a servant. Even in human form He was 100% God, and yet He didn't demand all the glory, the divine privileges and the other things that were due to Him as God. He offered forgiveness even when it wasn't deserved. He was loving, patient, honest, dependable, compassionate, peaceful, merciful and shall I go on?! These attitudes of Jesus are in stark contrast to the way I was and to the following phrases which are so common in today's culture: "do what is best for you," "if it makes you happy," "worry about yourself first," "that's my right," or "I will do what I want."

Like Jesus, do you humble yourself to serve others; or, do you find yourself wanting others to serve you? When you humble yourself, you have to put your rights aside and focus on the other person. When you do that, your attitude quickly changes. You focus on others' needs instead of what makes you happy, and *that* brings much greater rewards.

Matthew 5:5 NLT says,

> *"God blesses those who are humble, for they will inherit the whole earth."*

I encourage you to read Philippians 2:1-11 for yourself. These verses explain how we should behave and how to be humble. When we are truly humble our attitude changes. God knows your heart. He knows whether you are truly humble or just acting in false humility. You might be able to fool others, but you can't fool God. And neither can I.

1. Do you consider your attitude to be bad or good? Would others agree with this perspective?

2. When have you acted in false humility, such as going through the words and motions of concern for someone, but deep inside you really didn't care?

3. What first step do you need to take toward having a more humble attitude?

Authority

My mother said as a child, I never comprehended the meaning of "no". When she told me no, I whined, pouted and let her know just how mean she was for not letting me have my way! And to tell you the truth, I had a knack for wearing her down and most of the time she would cave. My poor mother.

Over time, this unhealthy cycle taught me that I didn't really need to respect authority. After all, if I could just keep pleading my case, I would eventually get my way.

As I grew up, the scripture in Ephesians 6:1, "Children, obey your parents because you belong to the Lord, for this is the right thing to do." didn't exactly sink-in. Fast-forward into my adulthood and naturally my problems with authority were still there. In the workplace I never wanted to accept "no" for an answer either. I would relentlessly plead my case and negotiate to get what I wanted.

But eventually, something changed.

I began to look at things differently when I began to recognize the truth about one man, a man named Jesus, God's son. He is the ultimate authority and I had to realize who I am in light of who He is! Bottom line: He is God and I am not. Matthew 28:18 NLT says,

Jesus came and told his disciples, "I have been given all authority in heaven and on earth."

This verse doesn't say "some authority"; it says **"all** authority." That verse put things in perspective. God is big—real big. I am not. In fact, I'm small. Why would I think I have the right to tell God, the CREATOR of the universe, what to do? Sounds nuts! Answer: because I presume I'm the one in control of my own life. Well, here's what I've learned: I'm not in control of my life—He is. Regardless of whether or not I like what is happening around me, God is still the ultimate authority, not me.

Even though God has ultimate authority, He has given authority to our governments, our parents and our church leaders to govern us. Jesus Himself practiced submission to authority. For example, in John 19:11 NLT it says,

Then Jesus said, "You would have no power over me at all unless it were given to you from above...."

In this scripture Jesus is talking to the Roman Governor, Pilate. Jesus, the Son of God, was delivered into the hands of the Roman government and was sentenced to death on the cross. In the verse above, He is expressing His accurate understanding of the order of authority and His willingness to submit to His Father's will.

So, how do we know how to correctly respect authority? The answer is to read the Bible. If God is the ultimate authority, then we need to know what He said. By submitting to His word, we practice a right understanding of the order of authority in our lives as well. 2 Timothy 3:16 NLT says,

All scripture is inspired by God and is useful to teach us what is true and to make us realize what is wrong in our lives. It corrects us when we are wrong and teaches us to do what is right.

1. Who are your authorities?

2. How well have you respected authority?

3. In your own words, describe how big God really is to you.

Bad Language

In my mind, bad language can be a couple of different things: cussing and tearing down others. Bad language seemed routine to me since my father used bad words very frequently during my childhood. And usually cussing was paired with tearing people down. It seems Dad thought cussing was the only way to get people to behave the way he wanted. While I never picked up the cussing habit, I did catch on to tearing others down. Why?

Because hurt people, hurt people.

But I have come to realize that I am responsible for my mouth. No. Matter. What. If others upset me, I am responsible for my response. People's actions do not dictate my reactions, even though it is easiest to place the blame on someone else.

Thankfully the Bible specifically addresses bad language and why it should not be used.

> *Let no corrupting talk come out of your mouths, but only such as is good for building up, as fits the occasion, that it may give grace to those who hear.* (Ephesians 4:29)
>
> *Let there be no filthiness nor foolish talk nor crude joking, which are out of place, but instead let there be thanksgiving.* (Ephesians 5:4)

Using bad language is not an encouragement to others and it isn't helpful! Ever.

Think for a moment. Would you rather be torn down or built up? I believe it is safe to say encouragement is preferred by all people. If you have been torn down, extend grace and forgive. Have you ever heard the phrase, "think before you speak?" One Sunday when my pastor was preaching he gave this T.H.I.N.K before you speak acrostic:

Is what you are about to say…(in person or online)…

T – True
H – Helpful
I – Important
N – Necessary
K – Kind

I challenge you to use this method the next time you start to speak negatively in any way. Is what you are about to say true, is it helpful, is it important, is it necessary or is it kind? If you answer "no" to any of those questions, I would encourage you to refrain! It will be hard, but it's worth it!

1. Do you have trouble thinking before you speak? How does the T.H.I.N.K. acrostic help you?

2. What does the phrase, "I am responsible for my response" mean to you?

3. Do you blame others for your reactions to them? (Ex: She made me angry, so I yelled at her.)

Bible

I went down to my basement to the bookshelf recently to look for a specific devotional book. I didn't find what I was looking for, but instead a few of my old Bibles caught my eye. Two of them had my maiden name inscribed on them and the third one had my married name on it. I picked up each one and began looking through them. I found things tucked inside from money to a postcard signed by Luke Perry from 1993. Don't ask me why I had that in my Bible because I wouldn't be able to tell you! Safe keeping perhaps? Going through my Bibles gave me a laugh, but it also stirred my emotions. Why? Because none of them looked like they had been used. They were dust collectors. One that I had received when I graduated high school was still in the box. During that phase of my life I was a casual reader. I would only read a few scriptures when I was struggling, and that usually consisted of finding them by playing Bible roulette. I would close my eyes, open my Bible and start reading. While this did work some of the time, this was not what I was supposed to do. I was not called to have a casual relationship with God; I am to be all in with God. This requires me to read and study my Bible, the living and active Word of God.

2 Timothy 3:16-17 says,

All Scripture is breathed out by God and profitable for teaching, for reproof, for correction, and for training in righteousness, that the man of God may be complete, equipped for every good work.

The Bible is breathed out by God. God inspired the writers by giving them the exact words to say. It isn't a book of fairy tales or a collection of stories, but words we should live by. It is profitable for teaching because it is the truth. We live in a culture of compromise, and the opinions of people are across the board. We can test those opinions by going to the Bible and receiving the truth. This is necessary! It gives us answers to life. It is also given to us for reproof, which is correcting wrong beliefs or behaviors (which leads to repentance). Don't merely take someone's word for what the Bible says, look for yourself! They could be wrong.

Correction seems like a tough one, but it isn't. It is gentle. When the Word corrects you, it is easily accepted. It is your instruction manual in life and provides training in a positive way. There is so much negativity in our society and when you read the Word, it is like a breath of fresh air. It is infectious. You want more of it. When you dig into the Word, you will become complete and equipped. If God tells you to do something, He will give you what you need to accomplish the task. It takes a lot of pressure away when we realize we don't have to do everything on our own. While the Bible itself may overwhelm you, take heart!

1 Peter 2:2-3 says:

Like newborn infants, long for the pure spiritual milk, that by it you may grow up into salvation — if indeed you have tasted that the Lord is good.

You aren't going to wake up one day and know everything about the Bible. Just like a baby drinks milk and slowly increases to solid foods, a Christian's spiritual growth takes time. Slowly you will mature in your faith, start to understand the Bible more and really get a taste of how good God is. You may not know where to start reading. Just start. God will reveal to you who He is and how He wants to shape your life.

1. How often do you read your Bible?

2. What distractions are keeping you from reading the Bible?

Birth

When I was growing up, I often wondered why I was born into my family. Nobody knew about my childhood hardships, not even my best friend. I would pretend to be somebody else in a different family, so the reality of my life wouldn't seem so bad. But, all my pretending bred jealousy. I became jealous of loving parents who were active in their kids' lives. Jealous of how loved and cherished they were. I wanted that more than anything! My struggles were deep, and my mom did the best she could under the circumstances with my father. It was even hard to have a good relationship with my mom when my father didn't allow it. We were a dysfunctional family. We fought. We yelled. We had no peace. There. Was. Little. Laughter. It was hard. I love my family and I know I couldn't choose the one I was born into, but I can choose now. I can choose to be born again into a new family. I'm not talking about physically; I'm talking about spiritually. John 1:12-13 says,

> But to all who did receive him, who believed in his name, he gave the right to become children of God, who were born, not of blood nor of the will of the flesh nor of the will of man, but of God.

Jesus chose you! He loves you. He wants you. But, you must choose Him too, to become a part of His family, which is becoming spiritually reborn. 2 Corinthians 5:17 says,

> Therefore, if anyone is in Christ, he is a new creation. The old has passed away; behold, the new has come.

This rebirth will begin to change your heart desires from your old ways to new ways that are of God. You become alive, spiritually. You become new.

You can start over! You may ask, how do you become spiritually reborn? Through faith. Believe in Jesus and submit your will to Him. When you do this, you become a child of God and will inherit everything He has to offer! On the flip side, Jesus said in John 3:3,

> Jesus answered him, "Truly, truly, I say to you, unless one is born again he cannot see the kingdom of God."

Life consists of a multitude of choices and accepting or rejecting Jesus is one of them. If you choose not to accept Jesus, you will not be born again and see the kingdom of God. This important choice in your life today will affect where you spend all of eternity. I am very thankful that I chose Jesus and I have never looked back! My childhood longings for a perfect family have been fulfilled in Jesus.

I am loved. I am cherished. And so are you.

1. Have you ever questioned why you were born into your family? Why?

2. Have you made the choice to choose Jesus?

3. What feelings well up inside knowing that being a child of God means to inherit everything He has?

Bitterness

Think of a time when you were angry or disappointed because you were treated unfairly. How did you respond to that person? At one point or another, everybody has been treated unfairly—hence the saying, "life's not fair." When I was treated unfairly in the past, I never acted appropriately. I would disengage emotionally from that person after I got mad and re-engage with my mouth by telling them what I really thought about it. Although sometimes I fail, I now choose to pray and let God handle it. For example, I had been hurt by some unfair circumstances. I was emotionally drained and literally laying on the floor asking God to pick me back up because I had nothing left. That next day at Bible study our leader pulled me aside and said she felt God wanted her to change the topic for the morning and that she believed this new message was for me. Wow. Just that was enough, but then she read this scripture from Isaiah 56:1-2 NLT:

> This is what the Lord says: "Be just and fair to all. Do what is right and good, for I am coming soon to rescue you and to display my righteousness among you. Blessed are all those who are careful to do this. Blessed are those who honor my Sabbath days of rest and keep themselves from doing wrong."

God says, "Look to me, do what is right and I will bless you." Shortly after, God gave me a mental picture of what he was doing. His hands were surrounding a ball of clay and He told me, "I'm working it." That confirmed to me that I had done the right thing by giving it to Him and He was working out my circumstances. I didn't need to say or do anything else. I went into my Bible study class that day emotionally drained and I left there with strength from the Lord.

Genesis 37-50 records the story of a man named Joseph. He was one of the youngest brothers of 12, and the favorite son of his father Jacob, which made his brothers very jealous. When Joseph was 17 years old, his brothers kidnapped him. They first plotted to kill him, but instead sold him as a slave to a passing caravan, which in turn later sold him in Egypt. Joseph grew in favor with his Egyptian master and was eventually placed in charge of the whole household. However, he was falsely accused by his master's wife of making sexual advances, so he was thrown into jail. Even there, he continued to do what was right. Eventually, God brought him before the Pharaoh and he interpreted a perplexing dream for this ruler. Pharaoh promoted him to reign over all Egypt, second only to Pharaoh himself. While Joseph was in this new position, his desperate brothers came to Egypt looking for food. The brothers were astounded to find Joseph in this new position of authority and power. Their shock quickly turned to fear that Joseph would be bitter about what they had done and have them punished. Joseph had certainly been treated unfairly. But, he chose to welcome his brothers and made a place for them to live near him. Joseph realized (read Genesis 50:20) that even though his brothers intended to harm him, God intended to use him. God had turned his circumstances around for ultimate good so that lives could be saved. We may not understand why we go through unfair and unjust things, but never forget that God can always turn things around for our good and for His purposes!

1. When you become bitter at a person, how do you respond to them? Do you show anger, revenge or gossip? Or do you pray?

2. Read over Joseph's story in Genesis chapters 37-50. Describe a time you felt betrayed or treated unfairly like Joseph was?

3. Forgiving others doesn't just benefit the person that you forgive — it helps you, too. Is there anybody you feel bitterness or resentment towards that you need to forgive?

Blame

I don't know about you, but I used to be the queen of blaming others for my actions. "If they hadn't done this, I wouldn't have done that." Nothing ever seemed to be all my fault and I would take the heat off myself and place it on somebody else. Sound familiar? I tried to justify my actions, but I was only fooling myself.

Blaming another person has always been part of mankind's sinful nature beginning with Adam and Eve after they initially sinned in the garden. Let's look at this story in Genesis 3:9-13.

> But the LORD God called to the man and said to him, "Where are you?" And he said, "I heard the sound of you in the garden, and I was afraid, because I was naked, and I hid myself." He said, "Who told you that you were naked? Have you eaten of the tree of which I commanded you not to eat?" The man said, "The woman whom you gave to be with me, she gave me fruit of the tree, and I ate." Then the LORD God said to the woman, "What is this that you have done?" The woman said, "The serpent deceived me, and I ate."

Did you catch the blaming by Adam and Eve? They knew they had done wrong but placed the blame on others for their actions. Notice something in these scriptures; God went directly to Adam and addressed him first. He didn't say anything about Eve; God wanted Adam to own up to his mistake. God didn't say "what did Eve do" or "both of you;" He said, "you." Adam responded by blaming the woman God gave him! Wow, that was a double whammy by blaming both God and Eve. Then, God went directly to Eve and asked, "What have you done?" And how did Eve respond? She blamed the serpent. They tried to fool God, but God wanted them to take responsibility for their actions, which they didn't do.

The point I want to make from this story is this: Take responsibility for your own actions and don't blame others for your response. I'm not saying this is easy. It is so not. Not blaming others requires humility and self-control, two things which are not part of our human-nature. They only come from God. Proverbs 28:13 says,

> Whoever conceals his transgressions will not prosper, but he who confesses and forsakes them will obtain mercy.

It is hard to admit when we are wrong, but confession needs to happen to restore relationships and integrity. When we can own up to our mistakes and stop trying to justify them we experience freedom. We discover freedom in knowing that we can't control people and how they act, but also a freedom in knowing that we can practice self-control in our circumstances.

1. Have you ever practiced self-control and owned up to your part of a disagreement? How did that make you feel?

2. How has placing the blame for your actions not helped your situation?

3. How often do you blame others instead of taking your time to think about your part in the situation?

Brokenness

Do you ever feel like your spirit is broken? Your world is falling apart, things are not going your way and hope is distant. When your season of brokenness peaks, you'll reach a point where you must choose between two different paths. One option is to continue traveling the same broken road and the other is to turn and be restored. The path you take is *your* choice!

I was broken for many years and didn't know how to get past it. I relied on myself and even on others to fix my problems, but any "solution" was only temporary. Let's be honest. We live in a broken society. Sadly, in all this brokenness we do little more than put a band-aid over problems, resorting to medications, alcohol, drugs, relationships, etc. to help us. The truth is these temporary fixes simply do not get to the root of the problem. The root of the problem is *sin*…which leads to brokenness…and when brokenness is handled incorrectly, it leads to yet more sin…which leads to even more brokenness. Get it? This is a cycle that will lead to destruction if it is not stopped.

The Bible tells a story of brokenness I would like to share. There was a woman who had a bleeding disorder for 12 years. Mark 5:25-29 relates her encounter with Jesus:

> *And there was a woman who had had a discharge of blood for twelve years, and who had suffered much under many physicians, and had spent all that she had, and was no better but rather grew worse. She had heard the reports about Jesus and came up behind him in the crowd and touched his garment. For she said, "If I touch even His garments, I will be made well." And immediately the flow of blood dried up, and she felt in her body that she was healed of her disease.*

I imagine this woman's spirit was broken. In her culture, she would have felt very isolated. Her medical condition was uncertain, and under Jewish law, the bleeding meant she had to keep her distance from others. So not only was she financially broke (having spent all available money on doctors), she likely had few friends and was not even accessible to her husband or children, if she had any. If she was married, this disorder would have been sufficient grounds for divorce (at least among the less conservative Jews). If she was not married, it would have prevented her from getting married. This desperate woman had no one and nowhere else to turn. But, one day she decided to go to Jesus for healing, and healing is exactly what she received.

This story of brokenness is no different than ours. This woman reached out to Jesus as the only one who could help her when she had nothing left. We serve the same Jesus today, and He can restore our brokenness if we give it to Him. Remember, turning to Him is your choice.

1. Have you turned to medications, alcohol, other people or even your own strength to overcome your brokenness? If so, did it fix it?

2. Have you been in the cycle of brokenness, either in the past or right now?

3. What would it look like for you to turn to Jesus for healing?

Busyness

I love to be busy, plain and simple. Some reading this may agree and say "me too" while others may think, "I don't like being busy; it stresses me out!" Honestly, being busy gave me a sense of accomplishment and purpose. Every morning I used to look at my schedule and knew it was going to be a good day if I didn't have 10 minutes to spare. My packed calendar left me with a feeling that I could conquer the world. The busier I was, the more purpose I felt.

During this season I was working full-time and had lots of evening activities. It seemed like my family was always running and I felt good about handling it all. But God had other plans. I didn't understand until I slowed down long enough to listen—by needing to have surgery. Who has time for that?! Two weeks off work seemed like torture, but God began to change my heart while I was still. He had my attention and told me to quit my job. What? I loved my job.

After months of prayer and thoughtful conversations with my husband, I put in my notice. Although I ended up working in ministry, I still went back to my normal habit of filling my calendar. Not having a full-time job gave me freedom to do what I wanted including ministry, carpentry and other passions. The problem: I was still filling my days. Sometimes I even used my busyness as an excuse to be disobedient. What God wanted from me meant I would have to be still. Well, guess what? I injured my shoulder, stopping me from doing the things I wanted to do (shocker, right?) and God slowed me down yet again.

Paul says in Ephesians 5:15-17,

> Look carefully then how you walk, not as unwise but as wise, making the best use of the time, because the days are evil. Therefore do not be foolish, but understand what the will of the Lord is.

Distractions are everywhere. Our grass needs cut, our cars washed, houses need cleaned, kids need to go to practice, gadgets need purchased, personal goals need to be met and our text messages need answered! We spend countless hours on social media, gaming, internet browsing, emailing and gossiping and our days are stolen. For what? Maybe temporary happiness or fulfillment, but distractions are ultimately missed opportunities. By staying busy, we miss out on all God has to offer us and we are detoured away from our true purpose in life—to serve God. Matthew 6:33 says,

> But seek first the kingdom of God and his righteousness, and all these things will be added to you.

God will bless you if you seek Him first! Ask Him what He wants you to do, when and how. What would happen if you were to allow God to take control of your schedule and you were obedient, whatever that looks like? This is only possible through prayer and reading the Word, so you can know what His desire is. Scripture tells us that God's voice is like a gentle whisper. To hear a whisper, you must be close. So, if you are too busy to stay still long enough to listen, you won't hear Him. You must draw near to God to hear and He promises to draw near to you.

My best "God moments" (times when He blew me away) were experienced when I was still, not busy. When people are on their death bed, they never wish that they had spent more time on their phone or wished their house was cleaner. They wish they had been closer to God and had made time for the eternal things that really matter. We don't realize how short our time here on earth is. Things I thought were important were just distractions. God has a plan and a purpose for you and living for Him is much more rewarding than anything this world has to offer.

1. What things fill your day? God, work, kids, phone, school, etc.? Prioritize them.

2. If you knew you were dying tomorrow what would you do differently?

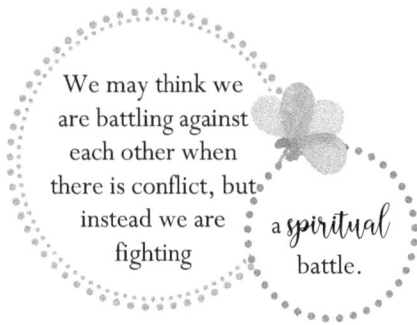

> We may think we are battling against each other when there is conflict, but instead we are fighting a *spiritual* battle.

Church

I often felt like a foreigner in the church I grew up in. I was rarely invited to teen gatherings and the few times I was, I felt the invitation was out of obligation. I am musically talented but can only remember twice in 18 years being asked to sing a solo. Those who were popular sang solos. I felt like I wasn't good enough to attend because I didn't reach a certain "status." As a child, I remember thinking that I couldn't wait until I was 16 so I could quit going.

Have you ever had a bad experience at church that turned you off from "religion" all together? Have you been hurt by someone attending a church? Have you been offended by a preacher? This is spiritual warfare and a misunderstanding of what "church" even is. Your enemy is also an enemy of the church and will use these hurts and anything else to keep you from entering the doors of a building where the people of God—the church—gather.

People sin, make mistakes and will definitely fail you. Guaranteed. But I know someone who won't fail you and who is perfect in His love toward you. His name is Jesus, the Son of God. He was born *perfect*, and He died *perfect* for you and me—for the church. *Jesus* is the reason we have church, is the head of the church and loves the church very much.

John 3:16-17 says,

> For God so loved the world, that he gave his only Son, that whoever believes in him should not perish but have eternal life. For God did not send his son into the world to condemn the world, but in order that the world might be saved through him.

God loves you and He wants you to have a personal relationship with Him. He wants you to focus on Him, His love, His grace and His ultimate sacrifice for you, and He wants you to do that alongside brothers and sisters in Christ. That is hard to do when our eyes are set on the faults of others, keeping us from this relationship that He invites us to enter. The Bible describes Jesus' intimate relationship with the church this way:

Ephesians 5:25 says,

> For husbands, this means love your wives, just as Christ loved the church. He gave up his life for her to make her holy and clean, washed by the cleansing of God's word.

Jesus sees the church as His bride and so should we. We may think we are battling against each other when there is conflict, but instead we are fighting a spiritual battle. Satan and his angels use such tactics as gossip, disagreements, pride, unforgiveness, bitterness, jealousy and slander to keep us from loving one another well and displaying the love of Christ. Does any of this sound familiar? But, that is not how it should be. People who claim to follow Jesus should certainly model their life after His teachings with the help and correction of the Holy Spirit, but we must understand that people will still fail, even in the church. Jesus extended grace to us when we didn't deserve it and we should do the same to people who hurt us.

By the grace of God, I didn't quit going to church. I shifted my eyes from the faults of others to the love of my Savior. While those past situations were hurtful, they helped me run into the arms of Jesus. In His arms is where I should have been all along.

1. Have you ever been guilty of not wanting to attend a church?

2. Have you ever found yourself trusting in people more than Jesus? Did they fail you?

3. What steps do you need to take to trust in Jesus more and trust in people less?

Comfort

I was very close to my maternal grandmother. She lived down the street from where I grew up, so I was at her house quite often. We would spend evenings sitting on the porch watching the cars go by and making up car colored games as they went. She taught me how to crochet on that porch, crocheting chains longer than the sidewalk, then pulling them apart and starting over. I have laughed on that porch as much as I have cried. Why was this porch so special to me? It may not be what you are expecting; it was because my grandma didn't believe in air conditioning or turning on lights! So the breeze was much nicer outside. Grandma always brought me to church. She became my mentor and was the one I asked when I had questions about the Bible. She was my safe haven when things were tough at my house. When I would stay the night at her house, our evening would go something like this: talk, a supper of corn flakes followed by vanilla ice cream dessert, then watch the news. All with the lights OFF—she made sure we didn't turn any lights on by taping every one of them down. Good memories. She taught me the simple life.

In December 2010, my spunky and funny grandma, the one I had relied on all my life, died. While singing "What a Day That Will Be" at her funeral, I longed for the day I could see her again. After the funeral I went home and on my knees in my bedroom cried out to God as I mourned my loss. While I was glad she had finally reached heaven as she had longed for, I felt selfish for wanting her back.

In Matthew 5:4 Jesus says this:

Blessed are those who mourn, for they shall be comforted.

The word "blessed" is referring to being happy by experiencing hope and joy. How could I be happy while I'm mourning? Because when Jesus died, God gave us His Holy Spirit. He is our Comforter and Advocate who lives within us after we accept Jesus. While I was on my knees in my bedroom that day, the Holy Spirit gave me a peace and a joy, stronger than I had ever experienced, so that my tears of mourning immediately turned into tears of joy. It was like I could feel the joy she was experiencing in heaven. I began to worship God and I knew that everything was going to be okay. He promised that I would be comforted, and He didn't forsake me. He won't forsake you either, if you believe in Him. It's been said, "Suffering makes room in our hearts to experience God's peace." When we make room for God, He shows up in a way that we can't explain or even comprehend.

Once we experience God's peace in suffering, we will often later find an opportunity to help others when they suffer. 2 Corinthians 1:3-4 show us this:

Blessed be the God and Father of our Lord Jesus Christ, the Father of mercies and God of all comfort, who comforts us in all our affliction, so that we may be able to comfort those who are in any affliction, with the comfort with which we ourselves are comforted by God.

Your suffering is not an accident and in due time will be used for good. You may not be able to understand it at the time, but you will one day—in this life or the next. Keep trusting in God and give praise to Him through it all. He is worth it.

1. How have you experienced suffering in your life?

2. Do you find it difficult to worship God during suffering? Why or why not?

Contentment

Growing up, my parents lived paycheck to paycheck. And sometimes, not even that! While I never went without necessities, I did compare what I didn't have to what other people did have, especially in school. I wasn't content with my life and I wanted more. I wanted to feel accepted. In my mind, I thought in order to be accepted I had to change. I tried to act different, more like the popular crowd and I wanted to wear certain brand-named clothes. Sounds vain, doesn't it? Well, it is. This. Is. Surface. Level. Stuff. Such a lack of contentment is often a symptom of a bigger root problem. The root problem is a void—a God-shaped void—deep in our souls.

In Philippians 4:11-13, Paul, a man known as one of the greatest followers of Jesus of all time, shares the secret of contentment.

> Not that I am speaking of being in need, for I have learned in whatever situation I am to be content. I know how to be brought low, and I know how to abound. In any and every circumstance, I have learned the secret of facing plenty and hunger, abundance and need. I can do all things through him [Jesus] who strengthens me.

Paul had a lot of highs and lows in his life. Like, he suffered unimaginable hard stuff. But, Paul recognized that no matter the situation, his contentment wasn't found in outward circumstances. Paul was not bothered when he wasn't accepted by others because his focus was not on others' approval. It didn't matter if he went hungry or if he was blessed beyond measure. His contentment was found in Jesus, and so should ours be. God was the one who gave him strength, and Paul knew that He would never leave him.

In 1 Timothy 6:6-7 Paul shares more about contentment:

> But godliness with contentment is great gain, for we brought nothing into the world, and we cannot take anything out of the world.

Profitable contentment is not found without godliness. Godliness is making God the center of your life and submitting to His will. You weren't brought into this world with anything, and you can't take anything with you when you die. So, make this one life you have count—live on mission by proclaiming who God is and what He has done for you! Life isn't about money, how many friends you have, what kind of car you drive, how big your house is or how the world measures "success." When you die, those things will have no significance. The only thing that will have significance when you die is the relationship you have with Jesus. Was the God-shaped hole of discontentment you were born with filled by God or did you mistakenly attempt to fill it with things of this world?

1. In what areas in your life do you struggle with contentment?

2. How have you attempted to fill the void in your life that only God can fill? Be specific.

3. Have you ever been completely content? Describe that time.

Challenge: Dig deep into the Word of God and watch the desires of your "wants" in this world disappear.

Control

C an I confess something? I like control. I like to control my life in every aspect—who is (or isn't) in it, what other people are doing, my kids' actions or how a project should be completed. When things don't go as planned, I get frustrated because even though I had a plan B, I preferred plan A. Do you know what all of this is? Exhausting. While society is screaming to me, "you are in control!" it is simply not true. I had to come to the realization after my exhausting attempts to control things, that I'm in control of nothing! Once I realized this, I had a different outlook. God is God and I am not; and He is the One who made me, as stated in Genesis 1:27.

So God created man in his own image, in the image of God he created him; male and female he created them.

I still find myself asking, "How could I tell God—the Creator of the Universe—how to do things or question Him?" It isn't my place, never has been and never will be. Accepting this truth was freeing. Freedom from the anxiety I put myself through when things don't go as planned or worrying about other people.

Philippians 4:6 says,

Do not be anxious about anything, but in everything by prayer and supplication with thanksgiving let your requests be made known to God.

Matthew 6:34:

Therefore do not be anxious about tomorrow, for tomorrow will be anxious for itself. Sufficient for the day is its own trouble.

To experience freedom from control, you must FIRST realize that you are not in control and that God is the ONE seated on the throne. You cannot allow God to work through you when you are still trying to take the lead. We simply cannot compete with Him. Second, make a daily, conscious decision to submit your own will and desires to His perfect will. This is easier said than done, especially if you try doing it in your own strength. Lean solely on God and watch those issues of control slowly vanish. Let go and experience freedom!

1. What are things you like to control? List them. How differently would your life look if you allowed God to be in control?

2. In the big scheme of things of God's plan, does the thing you are trying to control really matter? Or is it something that could be overlooked?

3. Why is it difficult for you to give up control?

Criticism

Have you ever heard the phrase: "the apple doesn't fall far from the tree"? This phrase proved true with me in being critical of others. My father was a very critical man and if something wasn't done right, yelling would quickly follow. In a home video from my childhood I was mowing a patch of grass to prepare for our new garden. Apparently, I wasn't doing it correctly because the video shows my father having the worst temper tantrum.

This type of criticism from my dad continued all throughout my childhood and I took the baton from him when I became an adult. I unintentionally continued this critical spirit. It's what I knew. I found myself criticizing actions of people because I felt like I could do them better. My criticism wasn't helping, it was making things worse. It tore people down and before I knew it, they didn't try any more or pushed me away.

Galatians 5:14-15 says,

> For the whole law is fulfilled in one word: "You shall love your neighbor as yourself." But if you bite and devour one another, watch out that you are not consumed by one another.

Love trumps criticism. Period.

It is easy to see the faults of others and difficult to love them through it. All of us can quickly turn to gossip and the good that we used to see in that person vanishes. When you start to become critical of a person, love them by looking at how much you love yourself. If you can dig deep and look at how you would want to be treated when you need help, it would be easier to show that same respect and love to another person. Put yourself in their place and think about it before you speak words that could deflate their spirit.

Living a life without love is like a pack of wild animals, biting and devouring each other. It will always end with one or both getting hurt. Why do animals in the wild fight like this? Because it's their nature. They each want something to benefit themselves and will consume each other to get it. It can be brutal! This is how having a critical spirit can be. When we criticize we essentially are devouring another person, for our own personal gain. We tend to not count the cost of relationships and are blinded by the battle within ourselves.

I have learned when my eyes are focused completely on God, I'm not as critical of others. Things don't bother me as much, but when they do, I pray about it. Things don't have to be done my way. I had to accept that people do things differently. And while their actions may or may not be wrong, I must learn the proper way to handle them: not with criticism but with love. Taking that step back and getting's God perspective on the situation at hand is difficult sometimes, but it has proven to be beneficial for all. I'm a work in progress, but by God's grace He is helping me defeat the cycle of criticism, step by step.

1. Who have you criticized?

2. How has criticism that you have received affected you?

3. What steps will you try to take before being critical of somebody?

Darkness

When I was a kid I feared the dark. My dad loved to jump out and scare me in our dark hallway or say that there were ghosts that were going to get me. If someone had been recording me, it would have looked like an action-packed movie. I usually had a plan for the hallway. My first instinct was to make a mad dash to turn on the light. My fear went to a whole new level if the bulb was out or if it blew as I turned it on! My second panic move was to get to the next doorway with my eyes closed and swipe for the next light switch. All this anxiety just to use the *bathroom*! Oh, why did the bathroom have to be in the hallway? If it wasn't my dad scaring me in the hallway, it was a sibling hiding out in the basement dressed like Freddy Kruger, chasing me right back up the steps. I wonder how I even survived. (Face palm)

Spiritual darkness can be overwhelming and fearful at the same time. Unfortunately, darkness is everywhere in this world and the Bible associates spiritual darkness with the enemy, confusion and sin. The enemy can bind us in many emotional or physical ways. Depression, anxiety, suicide, hopelessness, loneliness, divorce, abuse, adultery, pornography, drugs, alcohol and other addictions have darkened the door of people's hearts all over the world. But there is hope.

Darkness brings fear, but light brings comfort. John 1:5 says,

> *The light shines in the darkness, and the darkness has not overcome it.*

Acts 26:17b-18 says,

> *I [Jesus] am sending you to open their eyes, so that they may turn from darkness to light and from the power of Satan to God, that they may receive forgiveness of sins and a place among those who are sanctified by faith in me.'*

Please remember that the darkness of sin and evil will **never** be able to overcome the light. Light = Jesus. Jesus wants to come in and break down the walls of darkness in your heart with Himself. Just as light brings comfort to us in a dark room, Jesus brings comfort and hope to our lives. John 8:12 says,

> *Again, Jesus spoke to them, saying, "I am the light of the world. Whoever follows me will not walk in darkness but will have the light of life."*

The power of darkness wants to overcome you and keep you full of fear, but you don't have to walk in it. It is a matter of choosing Jesus who will light your path, guide you and deliver you from the enemy. Expose the dark by confessing your sins and trusting in Jesus to find your freedom. He is the Light of the world! Let Him in.

1.   What type of darkness are you currently struggling with? Depression? Anxiety? Addiction, etc.?

2.   Have you made the choice to trust in Jesus and allow His light to shine in the dark places of your heart?

The seed of
deception has you
bound. Locked in.

Deception

Have you ever been deceived? Recently, I spoke with a very nice customer service representative about upgrading my television service. I asked about upgrading because of issues we were having with our system and he agreed that we could upgrade with a small increase in my bill, in fact he kindly offered me a discount. Sweet! We set up an installation date.

The technician came to install my system and two hours later handed me paperwork to sign. The first page explained the job he had done, and the second page was an expensive 24-month agreement. A contract had never been mentioned so I was not happy. The tech and I called customer service and they spent a lot of energy justifying their actions. Turned out a contract is automatic with an upgrade, but they failed to let me know that. I felt deceived. The upgraded system looked good, it was desirable, but in the end it wasn't what I wanted and I was locked in for the next 2 years.

This is exactly how the enemy works in our lives. He tricks us and leads us into a trap. But, if we are paying attention we can be prepared to fight back. Not against each other, but against the enemy and deception and we must fight using weapons of spiritual warfare.

2 Corinthians 10:4-5 says,

> *For the weapons of our warfare are not of the flesh but have divine power to destroy strongholds. We destroy arguments and every lofty opinion raised against the knowledge of God and take every thought captive to obey Christ.*

These *weapons include the belt of **truth** (knowing what God says), **armor** (protecting your heart and emotions), **shoes** (standing firm), **shield** (trusting God), **helmet** (salvation by accepting Jesus) and the **sword** (Bible). These are weapons of spiritual warfare that help us win.

Satan and his demons are consistently working against you. Most people fail to ever recognize this truth because we don't literally see them or recognize their presence. But, stop and think about it. These attackers are very real. You have an enemy! They take you captive through strongholds, shame and accusations about doing the very things they convinced you to do. They use deception to steal your peace.

The enemy starts by planting a seed…a "thought" …in your mind. It could be a desire for a person, a new car you can't afford, an idea or a lie about who you are. Whatever the thought is, it will seem true, appealing and beneficial. This is where the rubber meets the road. You can water the seed and it will grow, or you can choose to throw it out. If you choose to water it, the thought will become your focus—the desire of your heart—and the thing you believe. Keep in mind that the seed is growing because you are feeding it in your mind. Eventually, you will have yourself convinced (deceived), you will make a plan and you will act on what you believe. The seed of deception has you bound. Locked in.

1 Peter 5:8 reminds us to be on guard.

> *Be sober-minded; be watchful. Your adversary the devil prowls around like a roaring lion, seeking someone to devour.*

When a thought comes into your mind, question it. *Is this of God or not? Will it produce good and expand the Kingdom of God, or will it be used for deception? Is this a temptation that will lead to sin?* If the answer is not of God, get rid of it. Refuse to be deceived. Let's practice. (For more details on these weapons, please see "Armor.")

1.   What current thought are you struggling with? Do you think it is true and from God or a lie from the enemy? Why?

2.   How can you be on guard from being deceived by the enemy?

Depression

D o you ever have one of those days, weeks, months or even years of feeling hopeless or alone? Your symptoms could be the fruit of many "root" issues including guilt, shame, the grip of fear or the inability to continue due to a deep, haunting wound. Comfort may seem beyond your grasp and you may even question your purpose or your identity.

I have experienced those kinds of days. I sometimes even act "cold" to the people around me during those times. I would rather stay in my own little world and not interact with anyone. Being nice and joyful seems to take out the last ounce of my energy! When I am discouraged during those times, Matthew 11:28-30 always comes to mind:

> Come to me, all you who are weary and burdened, and I will give you rest. Take my yoke upon you, and learn from me, because I am gentle and humble in heart, and you will find rest for your souls. For my yoke is easy, and my burden is light.

We are not a burden to Jesus when we are discouraged or depressed. We are not bothering Jesus when we tell Him our problems, nor does He tire of hearing about them. He invites us to rest in Him and let Him lift our burdens for us. It is much easier to give our "roots" to Him than to deal with them on our own. Our burdens can be a heavy load to carry!

Proverbs 12:25 says,

> Anxiety in a man's heart weighs him down, but a good word makes him glad.

How much does your anxiety weigh? I would say that it weighs as much as you allow.

1 Kings 18-19 relays the account of the prophet named Elijah who struggled with depression. He had 450 prophets of a false god named Baal killed, which made queen Jezebel very angry. She vowed to kill him, so Elijah ran for his life. He was tired, afraid and very discouraged. He thought he had nothing to live for anymore and begged God to take his life. He felt alone and was convinced God had abandoned him.

But God ministered to his depression by giving him rest and food and he continued his journey. The Lord showed him that he wasn't alone, even though he thought he was. Elijah heard the gentle whisper of the Lord which energized him to move forward with God's plans. Elijah's purpose wasn't complete. The Lord gave him the strength he needed to go on.

Sometimes our lives are like Elijah's. We experience discouragement and want to give up. But we must remember that our mission is not over. God has a plan and a purpose for each of us and the enemy will do anything he can to try and stop it. This can come in the form of discouragement, the accusation of unworthiness, fear, shame, hopelessness—you name it! Seek God and He will meet you where you are, pick you up and give you the strength to continue. Just rest in Him, worship Him through the struggles and He will give you what you need, just like He did for Elijah.

1. What anxieties are you currently experiencing?

2. What or whom do you seek when you are discouraged or alone?

3. What does the saying, "When you fall, get back up" or "When you fail, try again" mean to you?

Emotions

Have you ever felt like your emotions were like a roller coaster ride? Feelings can change in an instant from happy to sad and then back to being glad again. For example, you could be fighting with a person one minute and then the phone rings and you answer it with a smile on your face and a warm tone as if you didn't have a care in the world.

Vacations can be stressful for me. Feeling the sense of responsibility to make sure things go as planned and nothing gets left at the hotel can put me on edge. On a particular trip, everyone was tired, and my husband was also on edge from me being stressed. I would love to relax, but I just can't seem to make it happen. Even though I have help, I feel like I must get everything done on my own which leads to frustration. This reminds me of a story in the Bible about Mary and Martha in Luke 10:38-42.

> Now as they went on their way, Jesus entered a village. And a woman named Martha welcomed him into her house. And she had a sister called Mary, who sat at the Lord's feet and listened to his teaching. But Martha was distracted with much serving. And she went up to him and said, "Lord, do you not care that my sister has left me to serve alone? Tell her then to help me." But the Lord answered her, "Martha, Martha, you are anxious and troubled about many things, but one thing is necessary. Mary has chosen the good portion, which will not be taken away from her."

I imagine that emotions were running high for Martha that day. She was upset that Mary wasn't helping her like she thought she should, and she voiced her frustrations to Jesus. In this Scripture I can sense the patience Jesus had with Martha—He had to say her name twice. What He was about to say had great importance and we should pay attention as well. Jesus knew that she was frustrated, and He gave her the solution: *Himself*. This was not a suggestion or an opinion, but a *necessity*.

As we headed home from that vacation, I realized my teenage son seemed stressed as well. I made him sit in the back of the vehicle with me and I told him that we both needed some Jesus time. Sharing headphones, we listened to a sermon podcast and a sense of calmness came over that back seat. When the sermon ended, he proceeded to tell me how his stress went away. It was a complete change in us both. I told him that our actions changed because we sought Jesus when our emotions were high. We can't depend on our emotions, because they are always changing.

We can trust the unchanging Word of God. Due to the vacation, I had not read my Bible in 3 days. I was vulnerable. The Bible is our sword against the enemy's schemes and if we aren't reading it, we are much more susceptible to his attacks. We might begin to act out on our ever-changing emotions if we aren't grounded in God's Word. Just as Mary was soaking in everything that Jesus was saying, we should do the same. Read God's Word. Meditate on it. Soak it in. And be amazed at how your emotional roller coaster becomes much more relaxed. Enjoy the ride.

1. How would you describe your cycle of emotions? Like a roller coaster, small hills or flat land?

2. Do you currently read your Bible? If so, how often?

3. Does reading your Bible calm your emotions?

Forgiveness

I no longer had the opportunity to *settle* my unforgiveness towards him.

Scott and I got married when I was just shy of 19 years old. I was excited to start my new life with him, and I vowed that things would be different in my new home. I.couldn't.wait.to.get.out.of.my.house! I thought that when I moved out all the bad would just vanish from my mind and I could move forward with my life and not turn back. In a sense, I ran away from my old past, but I still harbored unforgiveness in my heart toward my father. Three weeks after I was married, my father went into the hospital and passed away at the age of 53. I no longer had the opportunity to settle my unforgiveness towards him. Honestly, at that point in my life I didn't feel ready to let it go either. I wish that I knew then what I know now about forgiveness, because I wasted a lot of time in my life. It wasn't for another several years before I finally decided to let go and forgive him in my heart. But, once I did, I felt freedom from the burden of it. Paul explains to us in Colossians 3:12-13 why we must forgive.

> Put on then, as God's chosen ones, holy and beloved, compassionate hearts, kindness, humility, meekness, and patience, bearing with one another and, if one has a complaint against another, forgiving each other; as the Lord has forgiven you, so you also must forgive.

How easy is it to accept forgiveness for ourselves but not extend forgiveness to others? Very easy. By grace, when we ask Jesus to forgive us of our sins, He does. Immediately. If we have made that step to ask for forgiveness, we are required to forgive others. Immediately. Just as Jesus does for us. Let's look at Matthew 6:14-15 to see what will happen if we choose not to forgive.

> For if you forgive others their trespasses, your heavenly Father will also forgive you, but if you do not forgive others their trespasses, neither will your Father forgive your trespasses.

Wow. That is deep. And hard. But it shows us how important it is to forgive. Unforgiveness harbors resentment and bitterness in our hearts that consumes us. You know what I'm talking about. Jesus wants us to be free from this and forgiving others by grace (when they don't deserve it) is what will cleanse us. You may wonder, though, how many times should you forgive a person if they continually hurt you? Matthew 18:21-22 gives us this answer.

> Then Peter came up and said to him, "Lord, how often will my brother sin against me, and I forgive him? As many as seven times?" Jesus said to him, "I do not say to you seven times, but seventy-seven times.

This is a lot of forgiveness! What Jesus was getting at in this scripture is that we should freely forgive. Always.

When you forgive, I encourage you to treat the person like they have been forgiven. The talk and the actions must match. When you truly forgive, most importantly, it restores your relationship with Jesus. I wasted so much time in my life with unforgiveness and I don't want that for you. Time is short. Forgive. You won't be doing it for the other person; it is for you and your relationship with Jesus. I'm praying for you.

1.   Do you have any unforgiveness in your heart toward another person? Who and why?

2.   Are you willing to release the resentment and be free from it? If so, please do it now.

Forgiving Yourself

Have you ever done something for which you feel you can never forgive yourself? Maybe it was a sexual relationship, not speaking up, an abortion, abuse, adultery or angry outbursts. One thing is common for everyone who struggles with this: continuing to relive the pain. It repeatedly replays in your memory and you can't forget. You suffer emotionally, feeling unworthy and unloved. Before you know it, the pain is making your decisions.

Imagine getting a stain on your favorite shirt. You buy every type of cleaner on the shelf to remove it, but your efforts are unsuccessful. This stain represents your sin. The stain of sin can never be washed away by our efforts. Removal of sin takes a supernatural solution: Jesus.

Romans 3:25 says,

Whom God put forward as a propitiation by his blood, to be received by faith. This was to show God's righteousness, because in his divine forbearance he had passed over former sins.

Jesus took all our sins upon Himself on the cross. He gave himself as the ultimate sacrifice and died in our place so that we could experience reconciliation with God. So when you trust in Jesus and ask Him to forgive you of your sins and then you turn from them, they are gone!

Romans 8:1-2 says,

There is therefore now no condemnation for those who are in Christ Jesus. For the law of the Spirit of life has set you free in Christ Jesus from the law of sin and death.

He does not condemn you for your sin but declares you not guilty! Scripture does not say that we must forgive ourselves. When Jesus forgives us we are completely forgiven. So why do we still need to forgive ourselves? We may know that we are forgiven, but don't feel forgiven. Guilt and shame do not come from Jesus. They come from the enemy who keeps reminding you of your past. The enemy may tell you that you are worthless, God can never forgive you, your sin was too bad to be forgiven or to just give up. He wants to paralyze you with his lies and keep you in bondage. When you hear these lies, remember James 4:7.

Submit yourselves therefore to God. Resist the devil, and he will flee from you.

This is how you fight the enemy when he brings up your past: submit to God. The enemy is already defeated! Counteract the enemy's lies with the truth of God's Word and through prayer. When you have sinned against a person, first go to God, then go to the person and reconcile with him/her (if safe). By going to the person and reconciling, the enemy's stronghold is removed. Accept and believe that God has forgiven you so you can live in freedom.

1. What sin(s) is haunting you from your past? Have you asked God to forgive you?

2. What lies have you been told from the enemy? What is God's truth?

God

D o you trust God? Sometimes people struggle to trust God because their earthly father was untrustworthy. Some dads don't keep their promises and trust is lost. Maybe your dad was not present in your life or didn't give you the love you needed. On the other hand, if someone had a great dad who was always present in their life and who loved them unconditionally, it may be easier for them to trust God.

Trusting a Heavenly Father can be difficult if rejection is all you have known. You may ask, "How could a Heavenly Father love me?" "How could I truly trust Him?" Hesitation is a natural response when you have experienced a difficult upbringing.

Trusting God was a challenge for me at first and I felt hesitant. I compared God to my earthly father, even though they were complete opposites. I thank God for His patience because He has never failed me. But sometimes the enemy lies to me, whispering I cannot trust God and trying to compare God and my earthly father. There is no comparison. Period.

Luke 1:37 says,

> For nothing will be impossible with God.

God is all-powerful. He can do anything! The verses before this Scripture tell us of the virgin Mary, the mother of Jesus. She had never been with a man and God gave her a perfect child, Jesus. We say that this is impossible, but not with God.

God is also all-knowing. Psalm 139:1-3 says

> O LORD, you have searched me and you know me. You know when I sit and when I rise; you perceive my thoughts from afar. You discern my going out and my lying down; you are familiar with all my ways.

God knows! He knows everything about everything and everybody. He knows your heart, your thoughts and even how many hairs are on your head (Luke 12:7). To think that God knows our thoughts can seem scary, but He is approachable. James 4:8a says,

> Draw near to God, and he will draw near to you.

God knows that we sin, but He still wants us to draw near to Him. He wants a relationship with us! He wants us to bring our burdens, hurts and struggles and lay them at His feet—condemnation free because of Jesus. He loves us.

1 John 4:16 (NIV) says,

> And so we know and rely on the love God has for us. God is love. Whoever lives in love lives in God, and God in him.

Did you notice the word rely? I love this. Reliance proves the confidence we can have in God's love for us and that we can trust Him completely. He will never leave us and will never stop loving us. No matter how much love you did or did not receive from your earthly father, it will never compare to the love that God has for each one of us.

1. How does your earthly father differ from your Heavenly Father?

2. While the characteristics of God mentioned is a short list, how can you know that God is all those things and more?

Gossip

Gossip is a hard and emotional topic for me. Let me begin by hanging my head while I admit to having gossiped about people. This is not something that I am proud of, but ashamed. I have hurt many people by gossiping. It kills their spirit and ruins their reputation. I find myself wanting to gossip when I have been hurt by a person. If I talk about them, I temporarily feel better by convincing myself that I did nothing wrong and it was all their fault. But it is wrong of me to even think that, for more than one reason. It is not of God. I need to take responsibility for my words. I truly don't like gossip, but sometimes I find myself doing it anyway. Before I know it, the damage has already been done. Gossip has ruined friendships in my past, which has forced me to learn the power of my tongue the hard way. Proverbs 18:21 confirms this by saying,

Death and life are in the power of the tongue, and those who love it will eat its fruits.

Paul addressed gossip in the church in 2 Corinthians 12:20.

For I fear that perhaps when I come I may find you not as I wish, and that you may find me not as you wish—that perhaps there may be quarreling, jealousy, anger, hostility, slander, gossip, conceit, and disorder.

Paul's concern was that the ways of the people of Corinth had been brought into the church. He did not want this for the Christians and wanted them to be set apart from culture. These negative characteristics come naturally to people, which the Word describes as our "flesh." In our lives, we bear fruit—fruit of the Spirit or of the flesh. Let's look in Galatians 5:22-24 to see what the fruit of the Spirit looks like.

But the fruit of the Spirit is love, joy, peace, patience, kindness, goodness, faithfulness, gentleness, self-control; against such things there is no law. And those who belong to Christ Jesus have crucified the flesh with its passions and desires.

Looking at the chart, you will see the drastic differences between bearing the fruit of the Spirit and bearing the fruit of the flesh, by comparing the two scriptures. There are no gray areas. The closer I am in my relationship with God, the more I display the fruit of the Spirit in my actions. Not in my own strength, but His. I will encourage you to not get caught up in gossip when emotions are high. It is **hard** to hold your tongue and it takes discipline. But it works out for the best, as said in Proverbs 26:20 NLT.

Fruit of the Spirit		Fruit of the Flesh
Love	⟷	Slander
Joy	⟷	Jealousy
Peace	⟷	Quarreling
Patience	⟷	Hostility
Kindness/Goodness	⟷	Conceit
Faithfulness	⟷	Gossip
Gentleness	⟷	Anger
Self-control	⟷	Disorder

Fire goes out without wood, and quarrels disappear when gossip stops.

1. How has gossip ruined relationships in your life? Be specific.

2. Looking at the chart, which fruit do you display in your life?

Hatred

Have you ever had to deal with a group of people who were just downright mean and you hated them for it? When I was in middle school there was a group of girls that were considered the "mean girls" of my grade. Girls feared them. They thought they were tough—and they were.

One day at recess one of the mean girls and her posse` approached me. Apparently, it had been reported that I said I loved her boyfriend in a Valentine's school newsletter and she wasn't happy. I was confused. I had not put anything in the newsletter, nor did I know her boyfriend. But, all she cared about was getting revenge and I was her target.

So, the fight began. She and her posse` mocked me for months, laughing at me in the halls while I sported a bruise on my face. I hated her before, but after our fight hate consumed me. She robbed me of my self-confidence, my worth and my peace. Nothing about it was fair; turns out the initials were two different people.

Later in life, after I accepted Christ, I realized why God says not to hold hatred in your heart.

Proverbs 10:12 says,

> Hatred stirs up strife, but love covers all offenses.

Colossians 3:8-10 continues,

> But now you must put them all away: anger, wrath, malice, slander, and obscene talk from your mouth. Do not lie to one another, seeing that you have put off the old self with its practices and have put on the new self, which is being renewed in knowledge after the image of its creator.

When hatred or malice consumes us, it takes control. Slander comes easily and we tear down the character of our offenders. If we are not careful, the desire to cause physical harm will be inevitable. When emotions are high, we rarely make wise decisions. Am I right? What is shoved down in our hearts comes out of our mouths and the damage is done. We may not even have remorse for our words or actions and even say that they "deserved it." However, we are all sinners and deserve…well… Hell.

Jesus came to earth and died on a cross for you, me, our neighbor and for the one you may hate. He took the punishment that we deserve so that we may have eternal life with Him in heaven. When you accept Jesus, He wants you to put off the old self with its practices and put on the new self. Out with the old (hate) and in with the new (love).

You can choose not to hate, but to love instead. Love covers all offenses. To love is to choose not to aggravate the offense so the relationship can be restored. There is not room in our hearts for both hatred and for God. It is one or the other, and I hope you choose God. God showed me how to love and my hatred for the mean girl eventually turned into prayer for her. I still think about her to this day, wondering where she is and hoping and praying that she found Jesus. God changed my heart and He is willing to transform your heart, too.

1. Is there hatred in your heart toward anyone? Be specific and give reasons why.

2. How do you deal with hatred?

3. How has acting on your emotions made things worse?

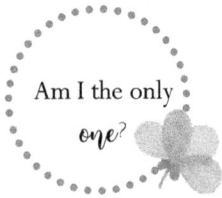

Judging

"Don't judge me." Ever heard that one before? While I honestly try not to judge people and show grace instead, I sometimes get caught up in it. Especially judging the ones who have hurt me. When I haven't fully been reconciled with a person, it is easy to judge the motives behind their behavior and I think like I am the one who has it all together. When I judge their motives, it puts division between us. But when I have a close relationship with a person, it is easy to apologize and forgive. Am I the only one?

When two people are divided, who is the source of the division? The answer is the enemy. The Greek word for Devil is Diabolos, which means "the one who divides." He is a false accuser, loves to sever relationships, loves to unjustly criticize and condemns with the purpose to destroy or hurt others. Read that last line again. Have you experienced any of those when you judge a person? Is the relationship severed? Did you accuse or criticize the person? Do you condemn? When we sit back and judge people, we allow the enemy to take a seat and be the director of the situation.

Spoiler alert—it will always end badly!

When I judge someone, the Holy Spirit always convicts me and asks, "What was your part in this?" Figuring out my part takes the focus off the other person. How can I accuse when I am guilty?

Jesus said in Matthew 7:1-5,

> Judge not, that you be not judged. For with the judgment you pronounce you will be judged, and with the measure you use it will be measured to you. Why do you see the speck that is in your brother's eye, but do not notice the log that is in your own eye? Or how can you say to your brother, 'Let me take the speck out of your eye,' when there is the log in your own eye? You hypocrite, first take the log out of your own eye, and then you will see clearly to take the speck out of your brother's eye.

It is easy to magnify the situation and place all blame on the other person and easier to excuse ourselves. We must own up to our part; when we do that, it humbles us. Reconciliation is easier when driven by humility. Let's try not to waste our precious time on earth with conflict caused by judging others. When conflict arises, trust in God to work it out within yourself and the other person and pray for each other. God is the ultimate Judge and we will all be judged in the end for our actions and words, as stated in Matthew 12:36:

> I tell you, on the day of judgment people will give account for every careless word they speak, for by your words you will be justified, and by your words you will be condemned.

Our speech reveals our hearts. So, I will challenge you the next time you want to judge and criticize another person, pray first. Ask the Holy Spirit to give you a new attitude towards this person and then let Him work. No one else knows our hearts and our motives like God does. Don't assume that you know, but trust Him to work it out.

1.   With whom are you experiencing division from being judgmental? What was your part in the division?

2.   How important is reconciliation? How does reconciliation (or the lack thereof) affect your relationship with God?

Love

Love was a word rarely spoken in my childhood home between my parents or siblings. I cannot even recall one time my father told me he loved me. As you can imagine, I never recognized what real love was. I know my parents loved me, but outward expressions of showing love didn't really exist, especially by my father. It wasn't until I met my amazing husband, Scott, at the age of 16 that I began to understand what real love looked like. Scott loved me for who I was. He respected me. He was kind. His love was the total opposite of what I had experienced. I could write this whole page on how amazing he is, but I will spare you! Looking back, Scott's love for me demonstrated how Christ loves us. Scott sought after me, found me in the pit, loved me through it and rescued me from it. I didn't have to become somebody else or act a certain way for him to accept me.

This is exactly what Christ does. He pursues every one of us, exactly where we are (usually in the pit) and then He rescues us from it—all the while loving us before it, through it and after it. This type of love is beyond us. Beyond our ability to perform or to comprehend, as stated in Ephesians 3:18-19 NLT:

> *And may you have the power to understand, as all God's people should, how wide, how long, how high, and how deep his love is. May you experience the love of Christ, though it is too great to understand fully. Then you will be made complete with all the fullness of life and power that comes from God.*

God's love is wider than we can imagine. It is so broad that it can cover the whole world and our multitude of sins. So, don't let shame or unforgiveness narrow your view. God's love is also long, longer than we can fathom. It is never-ending and goes from this life all the way into eternity. Jeremiah 31:3 states:

> *...I have loved you with an everlasting love.*

God's love has height by lifting us up to the heavens and has depth by reaching down into the pit to rescue us. So, when you are feeling unloved, discouraged, unworthy or alone, imagine the cross and experience the fullness of Christ's love. God's love isn't just a feeling, He IS love! John 3:16-17 says:

> *For God so loved the world, that he gave his only son, that whoever believes in him should not perish but have eternal life. For God did not send his son into the world to condemn the world, but in order that the world might be saved through him.*

God's unfathomable love was expressed in its fullness when Jesus died on the cross so each one of us could have eternal life. There are no limits on His love, nor does He pick and choose people to love based on their goodness. His love is for ALL! His love is based on HIS grace and HIS goodness. Know that He loves you, even when emotions have blinded you from the truth and you don't "feel" like it. God, who is love, never fails.

1. How has the love of Christ been shown to you through other people?

2. How can you put into words the love Christ has for you?

3. Do you need to work on knowing that Christ loves you, even when you don't "feel" like it?

Loving Your Enemies

Can I start by saying, "ugh"? This. One. Is. Hard! While I do not consider myself to be victorious in this, I'm better than I once was due to a growing relationship with Christ. Sometimes it is hard for me to love someone who has wronged me.

Why sometimes? Because it depends on where my eyes are fixed at the time. When my eyes are fixed upon myself, I have a pity party and allow the hurt to affect me. When my eyes are fixed on Jesus, I will not let it bother me because I realize it is not about me.

Focusing on Jesus allows me to love and extend grace to people because that is what Jesus Christ did for me. Before I came to Christ I was considered His enemy, yet He loved me. I am called to do the same, but I cannot do this in my own strength. It must come from Him!

Jesus teaches us about loving our enemies in Luke 6:27-36:

> "But I say to you who hear, love your enemies, do good to those who hate you, bless those who curse you, pray for those who abuse you. To one who strikes you on the cheek, offer the other also, … And as you wish that others would do to you, do so to them. If you love those who love you, what benefit is that to you? For even sinners love those who love them. And if you do good to those who do good to you, what benefit is that to you? For even sinners do the same. And if you lend to those from whom you expect to receive, what credit is that to you? Even sinners lend to sinners, to get back the same amount. But love your enemies, and do good, and lend, expecting nothing in return, and your reward will be great, and you will be sons of the Most High, for He is kind to the ungrateful and the evil. Be merciful, even as your Father is merciful."

Let that scripture sink in for a moment. Jesus said that we must love our enemies, do good to them and pray for them. That is the complete opposite of the world's teaching. Jesus understands that it is easy to love those who love you and difficult to love those who hurt you. Putting your emotions aside and loving them brings great reward! When someone tries to ruin your reputation, lies, gossips, or mocks you…love them. When you choose to love you are trusting that Jesus will take care of your enemies.

I would like to add that loving does not mean that you should have warm fuzzy feelings for them, it simply means to make a conscious effort to treat them with respect and do good to them, even when you don't feel like it. That warm fuzzy feeling may never happen, and that's okay. Be kind. Love. Show respect. I pray that God reminds me of this when I don't feel like loving the people who hurt me.

1. How hard is it to love the people who hurt you? Why?

2. When a person hurts you, how do you respond?

3. Would you be willing today to take a step of faith to be kind to everyone, no matter how you feel?

Modesty

Have you ever heard the saying, "It's what's on the inside that matters"? There is truth to this statement, but it probably is not what you are thinking.

Society has claimed this statement to mean, "It matters if they are good on the inside, no matter how they dress or look (good or bad)". Allow me to change this phrase to say: Who is living on the inside is what matters. The appearance on the outside can be a clear indicator of the heart's motivations.

When you get dressed do you think, "This will bring attention to me," or "This will bring attention to God in me." Modesty is a heart issue and your heart motivates decisions of clothing and actions! So who does your heart belong to? You or God? You cannot ride the fence.

1 Timothy 2:9-10 says,

> *Likewise, also that women should adorn themselves in respectable apparel, with modesty and self-control, not with braided hair and gold or pearls or costly attire, but with what is proper for women who profess godliness—with good works.*

1 Peter 3:3-4 continues,

> *Do not let your adorning be external—the braiding of hair and the putting on of gold jewelry, or the clothing you wear — but let your adorning be the hidden person of the heart with the imperishable beauty of a gentle and quiet spirit, which in God's sight is very precious.*

These verses are not saying that you should neglect your appearance, but to be aware of Who you are presenting to the world. Do you find yourself wanting to gain attention from the opposite sex by wearing clothing that reveals your body?

When you wear revealing clothing, you are sending the opposite sex a clear message: I don't respect myself, so you won't need to respect me; and I am not listening to what God is telling me about modesty.

God created women as emotional beings, including the need to feel loved. Dressing immodestly to gain "love" will only lead to brokenness. God created males as visual beings, and dressing immodestly can cause them to stumble into sin. When you cause that temptation by dressing immodestly, you have also sinned.

When God is the authority of your heart, your clothes and actions will reflect Him. You will carry yourself with respect and respond with a gentle and quiet spirit due to a continual growing relationship with God. THIS is what is attractive! Your desire to be "loved" will be fulfilled by knowing the love of God and you won't desire attention from others. Displaying self-control is a desirable quality.

Remember these things: Carry yourself with self-respect and others will respect you; and love God with all your heart! Attract quality, not quantity.

1. How has dressing immodestly given you attention by the opposite sex? Did they respect you?

2. Do you respect yourself?

3. How is dressing modestly a testimony of godliness?

Money

Back in 2016, God called me to quit my corporate job and my immediate thought was, "how are we going to make it financially?" When my husband and I sat down to look at the bills as a one income family, it was a little scary. Scary tight. We would be able to pay our bills, but by the skin of our teeth.

Right before Christmas that year, my husband's pay schedule changed from weekly to bi-weekly and let's just say January was a true test! Our income was drastically less than our bills that month and it was during that time, God sent me to a gas station to test my faith. As I walked in, a lady was just sitting there. Odd. I paid for my soda and overheard her explaining how she had nothing and was a long way from home. I gave her the last of my cash and quickly left. But, on my way home, God told me to go back, ask her what she needed and go buy it. Really?! I reminded God, yet again, of our financial situation, but He won. I took her to a local store and bought her what she needed. That night, we were blessed financially with a gift five times more than what I had spent on her! We trusted, God provided. God knows that we need money to live, but we should not depend on money nor have a love for it.

Hebrews 13:5 says,

> Keep your life free from love of money, and be content with what you have...

When you are content, you don't love money. You are satisfied. You don't desire the next best thing or covet what somebody else has, which is sin.

Matthew 6:21 & 24 says,

> For where your treasure is, there your heart will be also. No one can serve two masters, for either he will hate the one and love the other, or he will be devoted to the one and despise the other. You cannot serve God and money.

Our hearts follow our treasures. When we love something we invest our time, energy and money into it. Where and what you invest in reveals your true heart. Are you doing something for the love of God or to gain financial benefits? Do you get caught up in "keeping up with the Joneses"? Are you in so much debt that you are enslaved by it? When you are enslaved, the thing you are enslaved to becomes your master. It controls you. You find yourself working harder and longer to pay the debt.

Jesus warned us that we cannot serve two masters. We simply cannot invest in both Jesus and what money can buy.

1 Timothy 6:10 says:

> For the love of money is a root of all kinds of evils.

Money motivates us. You can get anything you want, or do anything you want, if you have money. Personal gain, opportunities, drugs, or sex are a short list of examples. They all promise happiness, but they fail us every time. The only thing that is lasting is a relationship with Jesus. Invest your time, energy, and money with a heart turned towards Him and you will see a greater return on your investment than anything this world has to offer. Your relationship with Jesus is the only thing you can take with you when you die!

1.   How has money (or the things it can buy) affected your relationship with God?

2.   Take an honest evaluation. Where and with what do you invest your time?

Obedience

O ne Thursday afternoon I was cooking lunch before I left to teach at my local pregnancy resource center. In that unexpected moment God told me that I was going to write devotionals. I don't consider myself a person who struggles with obedience, but writing?! That is a different story. Fear immediately came over me and I'm sure I was trembling.

I told God, "I can't do this. I don't like writing and I'm not good at it." He replied, "It is not going to be you that will be writing, it will be Me!" Peace came over me in that moment and He gave me further instructions.

Writing may not be scary to you, but it is for me. In fact, at times I have run from this very project. I would write and then take a long break like a bear in hibernation. I let my fear get the best of me, but God always brought me back to His calling. I found I couldn't run from God. I tried! There is no corner too dark, no schedule too booked or any place so far away that He can't find me.

One particular spring morning I was struggling with obedience. I had my running shoes on, ready to go. As my kids were eating breakfast, I opened my Bible to hear from God. I needed Him! My flesh was telling me to run, but my spirit was telling me to give my fears to God. I took my kids to school and when I returned home, I sat back down at my table to read more. To my surprise, the pages in my Bible were flipped to a different passage. Highlighted verses on that divinely appointed page jumped out at me and God spoke to me in that moment.

Those verses were Deuteronomy 28:1-2.

> And if you faithfully obey the voice of the Lord your God, being careful to do all his commandments that I command you today, the Lord your God will set you high above all the nations of the earth. And all these blessings shall come upon you and overtake you, if you obey the voice of the Lord your God.

Those verses hit me like a ton of bricks. Do you know what the title is for chapter 28? "Blessings for Obedience." Go figure, right? Have you ever heard the phrase, "God doesn't call the equipped—He equips the called"? I don't know who said this, but it is the truth. Sometimes we doubt our own capabilities and feel inadequate to fulfill our calling. Obedience isn't knowing all the answers and having everything figured out. Obedience is saying "yes" to Him and trusting every step of the way. You don't have to walk in your own strength, which is easy and natural to do; walk in His. Trust Him to equip you and surrender your will to His.

Luke 12:48b NLT says,

> When someone has been given much, much will be required in return; and when someone has been entrusted with much, even more will be required.

I need God's strength and ability to be obedient, no matter how hard it is. I consider it a privilege to be chosen by the Creator of this universe for His work. Think about that for a moment. I never want a time to come when He is silent because I have continually chosen to be disobedient. Time is short, so I challenge you also to choose to be the hands and feet of Jesus. Choose obedience.

1. Are you running from God? Explain the situation and the outcome.

2. What are your struggles with obedience? How can you overcome them?

Pain

I believe emotional or physical pain is one of the hardest things in life. Pain causes a person to seek help and comfort, sometimes from a good source like a doctor, a friend or Jesus; but sometimes from a bad source like drinking, using drugs to numb the pain or contemplating suicide.

Around 2011, I was diagnosed with a painful condition that had no cure. The doctor even told me, "Good luck on getting life insurance because they won't give it to you with this." I experienced emotional and physical pain and my quality of life seemed dim. I found myself doing the only thing I knew left to do—pray. I begged God for years to heal me.

One day I heard of a revival in town and I felt led to go. Nothing happened that night but as I got in my car, God told me to go back in and tell the preacher what I needed. I was hesitant at first, but I eventually went back in to talk with him. He prayed with me and was very firm with me to come back the next night. I told him that I didn't think I could because I was taking college classes that night. He was adamant.

The next night I went to class. My first class finished extremely early and my late class was canceled. Huh. I went home and decided to shower, but God spoke to me, firmly telling me to get out of the shower and go. I went even though I was late, and that night God healed me! No more pain and no more medication. My pain didn't turn me away from God; it brought me closer to Him.

In this life we will all have pain and suffering, but we must realize our pain has a purpose. The apostle Paul said in Romans 5:3-5,

> Not only that, but we rejoice in our sufferings, knowing that suffering produces endurance, and endurance produces character, and character produces hope, and hope does not put us to shame, because God's love has been poured into our hearts through the Holy Spirit who has been given to us.

We don't rejoice because of suffering, we rejoice in it. We are not alone in our pain and suffering because He is with us and the result is hope. When we overcome our pain with God, it draws us closer to Him and produces endurance. He uses these trials to produce character in us to make us more like Jesus. When we have that confidence, we will have hope that we can endure the suffering with the strength of God.

Paul endured a lot of pain and suffering in his life — more than we can imagine! He said in 2 Corinthians 12:9-11,

> But he [Jesus] said to me, "My grace is sufficient for you, for my power is made perfect in weakness." Therefore, I will boast all the more gladly of my weaknesses, so that the power of Christ may rest upon me. For the sake of Christ, then, I am content with weaknesses, insults, hardships, persecutions, and calamities. For when I am weak, then I am strong.

God may not remove your pain, but remember that His grace is sufficient. If you want to truly experience God's power in your suffering, give it all to Him. Pour out your heart in prayer and trust Him. Don't try to fix yourself in your own strength. True strength comes from God. Whatever pain you are enduring right now, remember this: He who brings you to it, will see you through it and carry you through it. He is trustworthy.

1. Look up Revelation 21:3-4. How does this scripture give you hope?

2. What emotional or physical pain are you going through in this season of your life? Are you trusting God?

Patience

We live in a society where everything is literally at our fingertips. If you want to know something quickly, you Google it—results come in less than half a second. If you are hungry, you go through a drive-thru where your food comes in 2 minutes. If you don't have the money for something you want now, you charge it. If you order products online, a lot of merchants offer free 2-day shipping, so you don't have to wait as long to get it. Employers push employees to work harder and faster and we even expect our kids to do the same.

Consequently, we have become an impatient society! I find myself doing a lot of these things for my ultimate convenience because I enjoy having things quickly. I have always considered myself an impatient person. If an idea strikes me, I want to start on it right away and not waste any time. I can train myself and others to act quickly, but that doesn't mean I can put God on my timeline.

Psalms 27:14 says,

Wait for the LORD; be strong, and let your heart take courage; wait for the LORD!

Sometimes I find myself trying to wait on God and then if He doesn't give me an answer in my time frame, I go forward with whatever I think is best…and I usually mess it up. Moving forward on my own actually implies that I don't trust His decisions. Ouch. Even though waiting for God's timing doesn't come naturally, His answer is worth the wait.

Lamentations 3:25 says,

The Lord is good to those who wait for him, to the soul who seeks him.

He is the One who holds all knowledge and wisdom, not us. And despite our actions, He is ultimately in control. Only God has the power to work out any situation for our good. But, being patient with God is not easy. But when you are faced with an issue or need direction in your life, I encourage you to be S.T.I.L.L.

Seek God in prayer.

Turn to scripture and meditate on it.

Ignore the advice of the world.

Let God work in His timing.

Listen for His answer.

God knows what you are going through and knows your circumstances. Lean on Him and wait for an answer. The answer may not be what you think—it will always be better!

God is so big that He holds the world in His hands. We can trust Him with decisions, our circumstances, and our lives. Nothing is too big or too small for Him. I have found when I trust God and wait for His timing it is always perfect and works out better. I even laugh about the way He works things out—He is brilliant.

1. How often do you find yourself trusting God and waiting for His answer?

2. How has being impatient made your situation worse?

I was not aware having to "walk on eggshells" in my childhood spilled over into adulthood

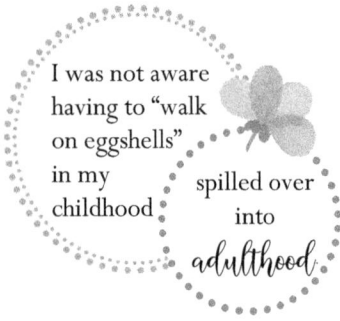

People Pleasing

Do you rely on other people for your happiness or feeling of self-worth? Do you find yourself being afraid to say no, tolerating abuse or unable to set clear boundaries?

I didn't realize I struggled with this until I was well into my adult life. I was not aware having to "walk on eggshells" in my childhood spilled over into adulthood. I couldn't say no to people because I wanted to make them happy. So, I would stretch myself thin for the comfort of others. But even though I was stretched thin, it made me happy because they were happy. God calls us to serve and love others, but *not* for the approval of men. We are not responsible for other's happiness.

Galatians 1:10 gives us advice on this topic,

> *For am I [Paul] now seeking the approval of man, or of God? Or am I trying to please man? If I were still trying to please man, I would not be a servant of Christ.*

Paul was a God-fearing, tell-it-like-it-is, gospel-preaching evangelist. I'm pretty sure if I was living in Paul's day we would have been good friends. (Just sayin'!) He didn't go around sugar-coating things and wanting to please others. He knew he didn't have to answer to people, he answered to God. He was on a mission, a gospel-filled one. Throughout the Bible, Paul showed an example of what an "audience of One" looks like by refusing to cater to the opinions of people and rejecting anything false. It wasn't a popularity contest to him; it was about being faithful to his calling. He knew he couldn't please people and please God at the same time. If he did he would be serving two masters, man and God. That would be like mixing oil and water—it doesn't work. I believe we can learn a lot from Paul and his walk with God by:

- Looking to God and fulfilling His calling. Don't worry about pleasing others because it leads to captivity. When somebody asks you to do something, ask yourself, "Is this pleasing the person or is it pleasing God?" **It is okay to say no!**

- Reducing busyness in life. Make time for God and take a sabbath day of rest. When you can hear Him clearly, it will be easier to say no to people and yes to Him.

1. If you struggle with people-pleasing, how do you plan on working on saying "no" to people? If you don't struggle with it, do you know somebody who does and are you willing to help them?

2. What priorities in your life do you need to change to reduce the busyness in your life?

3. What does an "audience of One" look like to you?

Pride

I struggle with pride from time to time. The Lord has given me talents and abilities and when that is mixed with my "A" type personality, the result can be pride.

In the past I had confidence that I had it all together, but when I messed up I danced around the topic because I could never admit it. The fault belonged to someone else and never me. I thought that tearing down others would result in me looking better. I was puffed up. I couldn't admit defeat because thought that would be viewed by others as weakness. *I was wrong*. This is what God has taught me:

Proverbs 16:18,

> *Pride goes before destruction, and a haughty spirit before a fall.*

James 4:6,

> *But he gives more grace. Therefore, it says, "God opposes the proud but gives grace to the humble."*

Have you ever been so prideful that you thought you were invincible and no one could touch you? You will eventually fall in one of two ways: Hurtful destruction or humble repentance. When you repent, you are recognizing God's grace and how much you *need* Him. You can't fall when you are already on your face before God!

Philippians 2:3 shows us one way to humility.

> *Do nothing from selfish ambition or conceit, but in humility count others more significant than yourselves.*

This verse isn't saying you should put yourself down. You are valued by God. It means that you should lay aside your selfish pride and treat others respectfully. Pride prevents you from having strong relationships where you can know people on a deeper level. When you are filled with pride, there is no room for anyone else—especially God.

Jesus said in Matthew 5:5:

> *Blessed are the meek, for they shall inherit the earth.*

Meekness is not weakness. It is strength under control. Admitting you are wrong can seem scary, but it will show you how much God's grace is needed because *no one* is perfect! This lifts God up, not ourselves. It is scarier to remain filled with pride and unable to grow spiritually.

John 3:30 says,

> *He must increase, but I must decrease.*

The high position of worship belongs to God alone. Worship is recognizing God for Who He is as you decrease. Insecurities fade as you fulfill your purpose through worship. When I started lifting God higher, things began to change. My pride was forced to decrease. I grew closer to God, was able to admit when I was wrong, began extending grace to others and became less likely to criticize or condemn.

1. In what area of your life do you struggle with pride?

2. Is there a person who you wronged that needs an apology from you? Who and why?

Repentance

I remember several years ago when I was driving on a highway with a median down the middle and I realized I needed to be on the other side. I was headed in the wrong direction. I decided to make a U-turn when the opportunity was available. I had my mother-in-law with me and she got a little nervous when I whipped the car around and pointed out the "no U-turn" sign that was posted. Seems like I wasn't the only one who had taken this route!

This story reminds me of our lives and our need to make U-turns. Just like my mother-in-law was nervous when I made such a drastic move, culture also gets nervous when we declare we are headed in the wrong direction. See, culture tells us that the wrong way is just fine. As long as what we are doing is "fun" or "feels right" it's "no big deal." While our choices may seem like fun or no big deal at the time, if they are against God, the "fun" will fade quickly. The pleasures and promises of this world will never bring us the joy and fulfillment that Christ gives; but gaining what Jesus offers requires repentance. Repentance is taking ownership of your sin and turning away from it—like a U-turn. You must change your mind, agree with God and reroute your life.

2 Corinthians 7:10 says,

For godly grief produces a repentance that leads to salvation without regret, whereas worldly grief produces death.

Godly grief is experiencing sorrow for your sin, which leads to making that U-turn toward Christ for salvation. Worldly grief is feeling bad about sin because it caused negative effects, but you don't go to Christ for forgiveness, which produces death. It would be like continuing to travel down a wrong road with no lights and your car runs out of gas. You have two choices: stay there in the dark or turn toward the street-lights in the distance. Which option would you choose?

Jesus said in Acts 26:17-18,

… I am sending you to open their eyes, so that they may turn from darkness to light and from the power of Satan to God, that they may receive forgiveness of sins…

You have the choice of a U-turn in your life that leads to salvation. You can make that U-turn away from the power of darkness to the light of God and live eternally. You may be nervous to turn your life around due to what others may think or say. You've seen the "no U-turn" signs the world holds up. Perhaps the shame of your sin keeps you from turning to God and you are afraid that He won't be happy with you because of your choices.

Jesus said in Luke 15:10,

Just so, I tell you, there is joy before the angels of God over one sinner who repents.

God seeks you out of the darkness with no condemnation. Heaven rejoices when you turn to Him! God is gracious, willing and able to forgive you because of the sacrifice Jesus made. Your sins are paid for. Just make that U-turn. If you have already rerouted your life but have strayed, I encourage you to return. The Father's arms are wide open—celebrating your return!

1. What does repentance mean to you?

2. Have you made the choice to turn to Christ for the forgiveness of your sin?

3. Has shame kept you from turning to Christ? Why or why not?

Salvation

I have attended church since I was two years old. As a teen, I thought I was a good person and considered myself a good Christian. I attended all the youth activities, was at church every time it was open, went to camp, tried to live a good life and talked to people about Jesus, but one thing was missing—Jesus.

Even though I was doing all those things, my *relationship* with Jesus wasn't there. *Please hear me when I say that going to church and having a relationship with Jesus are two different things!* Don't get confused. Going to church, doing good things, or being "good enough" won't give you a free ticket to Heaven.

In Matthew 7:21-23 Jesus said,

> *Not everyone who says to me, 'Lord, Lord,' will enter the kingdom of heaven, but the one who does the will of my Father who is in heaven. On that day many will say to me, 'Lord, Lord, did we not prophesy in your name, and cast out demons in your name, and do many mighty works in your name?' And then will I declare to them, 'I never knew you; depart from me, you workers of lawlessness.'*

Did you catch, *I never knew you*, in this Scripture? Jesus is after *you* and your *heart*! To get to Heaven, you **must** have a relationship with Him, accepting Him as Savior during your time on earth. Period. **There is no. other. way.** We must first know that we need Him.

Romans 3:23 says,

> *For all have sinned and fall short of the glory of God.*

Do you consider yourself a "good" person like I did? We will never be good enough to enter Heaven on our own merits. We will miss the mark every time. It is in our nature to do wrong, and that is sin. Lying, murder, pride, hatred, jealousy, adultery, idolatry (putting anything above God), disobedience, taking God's name in vain, disobeying your parents, anger, stealing, gossiping, lust and unbelief make up just a short list of sins. Have you ever been guilty of any of these? We cannot live up to God's standard because of our sinful nature. We are born that way.

Romans 3:10 says,

> *As it is written: None is righteous, no, not one.*

If you continue reading in verses 11-18, you will see that none are innocent. We easily sin through our thoughts, actions and words.

Romans 5:12 continues,

> *Therefore, just as sin came into the world through one man, and death through sin, and so death spread to all men because all sinned.*

Because of Adam's sin and our resulting sin nature, we are all sentenced to death and separation from God. We are all descendants of Adam. It's in our DNA and we need the Savior.

Romans 6:23 says,

> *For the wages of sin is death, but the free gift of God is eternal life in Christ Jesus our Lord.*

You may be wondering, "Is sin so big a deal that it should require death as its penalty?" Yes! God is holy and will not wink at sin. The Bible says he cannot even look upon sin. But, there is HOPE through His free gift!

Romans 5:8 says,

> *But God shows his love for us in that while we were still sinners, Christ died for us.*

At no point did we ever have to be "good enough" for God to love us. He loves you exactly the way you are. You don't have to wait until you "feel" like you are a better person, or your life is together for Him to love you. **He. Meets. You. Where. You. Are.** But He provides a way to get us beyond where we are, too.

John 3:16 says,

> *For God so loved the world, that he gave his only Son, that whoever believes in him should not perish but have eternal life.*

Romans 10:9-10 continues,

> *If you confess with your mouth that Jesus is Lord and believe in your heart that God raised him from the dead, you will be saved. For with the heart one believes and is justified, and with the mouth one confesses and is saved.*

God loves us so much that He sent His own Son to die on a cross to pay the penalty for our sins. He rose again from the grave three days later, defeating death. Jesus made a way for all of us to live eternally in Heaven through His death on the cross. Not by works or being good enough, but by believing in Him in your heart. This is salvation and the only way to Heaven. When we accept Jesus as our Savior, we are *justified*—God looks at you just as if your sin never happened. Salvation is not just for a select group, it is offered to everyone.

Romans 10:13 says,

> *For "everyone who calls on the name of the Lord will be saved."*

Don't listen to the lie that says you are not good enough for God and your sins are too great to be accepted by Him. When you acknowledge your need for forgiveness, He will wipe away all your sin. Sometimes we try to make this complicated, but it isn't. It truly is asking God to forgive you of your sins and asking Him to come into your heart. Simple. But, you must *believe with your heart*, not just say mere words. When you believe in something or somebody, you are passionate and your life changes.

After attending church all my life, I finally accepted Jesus in my early 20's. After a Sunday sermon, I was convicted about my sin and felt like I was carrying a heavy weight all week. I knew that if I died I would not go to Heaven and for the first time it really scared me. I had known *about* God all my life, but I had never put my complete faith in Him and I didn't really *know Him*. I did not have a personal relationship with Him. What I did have was a God-shaped void in my life, emptiness, and nothing else was able to fill it. Being the "good" wife I thought I needed to be, I was sitting on my bed about 10:00 p.m. that Friday night, waiting for my husband to come home from a late shift and I *finally* surrendered my life completely to Jesus. Best decision I've ever made. Easily.

If you have not accepted Jesus as your Savior, I would love to help you. I encourage you to pray the following prayer; similar to the one I prayed, and mean it in your heart to experience the joy of salvation! The power of salvation is not in words you pray, but in what God is doing in your heart. He will save you. Let these be your heart's cry to Jesus:

Jesus, I am broken and I know that I am a sinner. I can't go on anymore with the burdens of my sin. The load is too much. I am so sorry. Please forgive me of all the things I have done wrong and come into my heart. I want You to be Lord over my life and take control. I am declaring now with my mouth that I believe that You came to earth, died on the cross and rose again so that I can have a relationship with God. I trust you with my heart and with my life and I am completely surrendering everything. I pray that you would fill me now with your Holy Spirit and change me. Thank you for saving me. Amen.

Once I prayed, surrendering my life to Jesus, I cried. The joy and peace I experienced was overwhelming and in a good way. It was a totally new experience and I was a new person. In that moment, God made me a new creation, adopting me into His family and I was excited to proclaim Jesus to anyone who would listen. I want everyone to experience the grace of God, including YOU. Jesus chose to sacrifice His life so that we could have real life with Him. Truly, there is power in His name!

1. If you have already experienced salvation through faith in Jesus, when did you make this decision? If not before reading this, have you now prayed to accept Him?

2. How did your heart change after you accepted Jesus? If you have not accepted Jesus, what is keeping you from a relationship with Him?

Self-Esteem

How many times have you felt like you are not enough? You aren't attractive enough or skinny enough or smart enough. Have you ever wondered how anyone could even like you because maybe you have a little extra fluff or maybe you don't have enough? There have been times when I've gotten a little down about myself, so I did what most girls do—cried and ate chocolate! Sounds good, right? Well, it's not. I was listening to a lie that was whispered to me by the enemy. Believing the lie that I wasn't good enough was like looking through a distorted lens. I let my past and what people had said affect my self-esteem, so I had to combat these lies with truth! I had to look to scripture to understand what God thinks of me, not others.

- First, we see in Genesis 1:27 that you were created in HIS image.
  So, God created man in his own image, in the image of God he created him; male and female he created them.
- God created and knew you even before you were born! Only God could create you. Psalm 139:13-14 says,

  For you formed my inward parts; you knitted me together in my mother's womb. I praise you, for I am fearfully and wonderfully made. Wonderful are your works; my soul knows it very well.
- You are valued by God! Luke 12:6-7 says,
  Are not five sparrows sold for two pennies? And not one of them is forgotten before God. Why, even the hairs of your head are all numbered. Fear not; you are of more value than many sparrows.

God does not make mistakes with anything or anybody. You. Are. One. Of. A. Kind! You are cherished. You are loved. You are valued. You have purpose. I could go on and on about what you are to Him. But, one thing that you are not allowed to do is label yourself because God has already done that. You were created in HIS image so when you believe the lies of no self-worth, what does that say about God? What does that say about what you really believe about God? Just remember that you are fearfully and wonderfully made when the enemy tries to tell you lies about your value. God is fully aware of what happens to a sparrow and you are more valuable to God than a whole flock of birds! He knows you so well that He even knows how many hairs are on your head—and He loves all of you. He is invested in you, so believe Him. Be who God created you to be.

1. How has God defined you?

2. When you start questioning your worth, what thought or person triggers this? Is there truth to this? Does it agree or disagree with scriptures?

3. What truth about yourself do you need to work on?

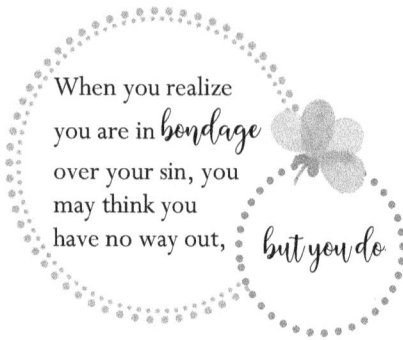

When you realize you are in *bondage* over your sin, you may think you have no way out, *but you do*

Sin

Have you ever done something and immediately regretted it? Or how about you knew something was wrong and you did it anyway? I've been there and done that so many times, too many to count. Sin is rebellion against God. God is completely perfect, and sin separates us from Him. Some people think sin is no big deal and view it as innocent, fun, desirable, okay if it doesn't hurt anyone or okay as long as you don't get caught. These are lies from the enemy and believing the enemy's lie creates distance between you and God.

Isaiah 59:2 says,

> But your iniquities have made a separation between you and your God, and your sins have hidden his face from you so that he does not hear.

Sin is dangerous. It has consequences. It is destructive. And according to Romans 6:23, sin leads to death. There is a reason people say, "If you play with fire, you will get burned." If only one sin keeps us from a relationship with God, it *is* a big deal. Not only that, sin will steal your joy.

Psalm 51:12:

> Restore to me the joy of your salvation and uphold me with a willing spirit.

King David wrote this after committing adultery with Bathsheba, finding out she was pregnant and then having her husband killed to cover it up. He sinned against God and the baby died. His sin produced more sin and resulted in his misery and brokenness. He acted upon the desire of his heart—aka: his feelings—and suffered major consequences, guilt and a loss of joy.

John 8:34 says,

> Jesus answered them, "Truly, truly, I say to you, everyone who practices sin is a slave to sin."

According to Jesus, sin is so powerful you not only lose your joy over it, you become a slave to it. It can produce so much fear you find yourself sinning more and more to cover up the first sin, just like David did. Before you know it, you are totally trapped in your own mess. When you realize you are in bondage over your sin, you may think you have no way out, but you do. Jesus is the way. He can immediately break chains of bondage if *you* confess your sin to Him and stop doing it.

1 John 1:9 says,

> If we confess our sins, he is faithful and just to forgive us our sins and to cleanse us from all unrighteousness.

2 Corinthians 3:17 continues,

> Now the Lord is the Spirit, and where the Spirit of the Lord is, there is freedom.

Jesus is the only one who can give freedom, peace and restore your joy. This requires confession of our sins to Jesus and asking for forgiveness. You'll be amazed at how quickly this freedom from bondage is given when you turn to Him.

1. What sins are currently holding you in bondage?

2. Has Jesus delivered you from the bondage of sin?

Social Media Acceptance

Have you ever had a love-hate relationship? That is what social media is for me. I love seeing pictures posted of families and reading the cute things kids say. You know, the happy things.

But I don't like the negative effects of social media. It can rob you of your time, cause conflicts or start gossip. The big effect, and the one no one wants to admit, is that it can cause you to seek your purpose and worth from other people's opinions. I loved social media, but in January 2018 I took a sabbatical from it. Not only was it a distraction, it occupied a lot of my time, caused anxiety and developed into spiritual warfare. It wasn't worth it!

Some seek their identity and worth from social media and don't realize it. People want to be *validated* (in their thinking) by venting or *accepted* by their "selfies" or "Ego portraits". Non-validation or non-acceptance, fuels depression, jealousy, anger, comparison, insecurities, eating disorders or even suicidal thoughts! We are basing our worth on how many "likes" our *filtered* picture gets, how many followers we have and how many people agree with us. It is becoming all about numbers—the more we have, the more we must be *worth*. People are assuming that if we "think" or "feel" a certain way (such as pertaining to our worth) it must be true. But our feelings and emotions do not define truth, God does.

John 14:6a says,

> Jesus said to him, "I am the way, and the truth, and the life."

If you start to question your purpose or direction in life, remember that Jesus is the way. When you are being fed lies about your worth, remember that Jesus is the truth. When you question if life is worth living, remember that Jesus is the life. Jesus is everything you will ever need!

Philippians 4:8-9 says,

> Finally, brothers, whatever is true, whatever is honorable, whatever is just, whatever is pure, whatever is lovely, whatever is commendable, if there is any excellence, if there is anything worthy of praise, think about these things. What you have learned and received and heard and seen in me—practice these things, and the God of peace will be with you.

Have you ever heard the phrase, "garbage in, garbage out"? What we fill our minds with will come out in our actions and words. If social media is causing you to "feel" unworthy or insecure, you will start acting on those "feelings."

God wants us to *listen* to the truths of His Word, but also *practice* them. We must counteract the lies with truth, believing and acting on the truth. Acting on truth is rejecting lies. Social media is not an avenue to find acceptance. Jesus is the only way to find true acceptance and love. It does not matter what others think. You will never be cast out or rejected by Him. Seek the way. Seek the truth. Seek the life. Seek Jesus.

1. Have you tried to find acceptance through social media? Take an honest evaluation.

2. On a scale from 1 to 10 (10 being the most influence), how important is a social media "like" to you.

3. What lies are you believing from social media? How will you counteract these lies with truth?

Spiritual Warfare

All of us are born into a physical world, but there is also a spiritual realm we cannot see. There is a spiritual battle going on—a war for our hearts. We don't see this war going on with our eyes, but we certainly experience the effects of it in our physical world. Unforgiveness, fear, pride, broken relationships, doubt, low self-esteem, hopelessness, instability, anger and mental exhaustion make up a short list of effects from the battles we face.

Ephesians 6:12 gives us the source:

For we do not wrestle against flesh and blood, but against the rulers, against the authorities, against the cosmic powers over this present darkness, against the spiritual forces of evil in the heavenly places.

The spiritual forces of evil have a goal: to steal, kill and destroy. The main goal is to destroy your credibility, your relationships, your hope, your health and your joy. We aren't battling against *each other*, we are battling the enemy. The enemy is a liar and will attack at every opportunity.

James 4:7-8,10 says,

Submit yourselves therefore to God. Resist the devil, and he will flee from you. Draw near to God, and he will draw near to you. Cleanse your hands, you sinners, and purify your hearts, you double-minded. Humble yourselves before the Lord, and he will exalt you.

How are we supposed to submit to God? First, we must YIELD. When we are attacked, it becomes all about us. We must be willing to trust God completely and allow Him to lift the burdens of our hearts, not taking matters in our own hands. We must firmly believe God is in control and trust He will handle our circumstances.

Another way of submitting to God is truly repenting of your sins. Own up to them! You can't have a close relationship with God if you deny your sins. Confess them and get *real* with God. The hardest part of submitting to God is humbling yourself with the truth of your great need for Him and through worship. Shift your eyes from yourself to God by exalting Him! Works. Every. Time.

How do you resist the devil? *Don't* give in to the lies and the temptations the enemy throws at you. For example, when somebody hurts you, don't give in to the temptation to retaliate. Give it to God in prayer. He is your peace.

Understand that you cannot fight the enemy on your own. God can! We are not strong or smart enough. God is! The war has already been won! When I'm in a spiritual battle, I like to go for a walk by myself. Listening to worship music and praying focuses my heart and mind on Jesus. When I do this, I'm completely trusting in Jesus to fight for me. By the end of the walk, I find myself no longer suppressed by the enemy. For you it may not be a walk. It may be a car ride, hiding out in the bathroom for 10 minutes or going to a certain room in your house. Wherever your getaway place is, fight the enemy with prayer, meditate on the Word and submit to God—in *all* things!

1. What type of warfare are you currently experiencing?

2. How do you currently handle this warfare? Does it line up with James 4:7-8?

3. Do you have a getaway place to pray? Where?

Temptation

I received an email recently from a very large auction company that said, "… has something to tempt you." I rolled my eyes and then deleted the email without reading further. Then curiosity got the best of me. I knew that whatever they were trying to tempt me with wasn't bad, so I went to my trash and opened the email.

There was no text within the email, only pictures consisting of a range of items from cars to clothes to televisions. The items were appealing to the eye and enticing. My immediate thoughts were, "temptation really is everywhere and in everything." It is in your email, your local shopping stores, television, social media sites, apps, search engines and even in your text messages. It doesn't matter if you wanted to see it or not, it's there. This can range from the "too-good-to-be-true" shopping sales to pornography. One thing is for certain, once your eyes have seen it, the seed of temptation will begin to work within you.

We know, as stated in James 1:13-16, that temptation is not from God.

> Let no one say when he is tempted, "I am being tempted by God," for God cannot be tempted with evil, and he himself tempts no one. But each person is tempted when he is lured and enticed by his own desire. Then desire when it has conceived gives birth to sin, and sin when it is fully grown brings forth death. Do not be deceived, my beloved brothers.

1 John 2:16 continues,

> For all that is in the world—the desires of the flesh and the desires of the eyes and pride of life—is not from the Father but is from the world.

In the beginning, Satan tempted Eve with the fruit that was pleasing to the eye. When she gave in to the temptation, it birthed sin in all of us. The enemy continues to do the same thing with us daily. Temptation looks innocent at first, but it will always lead to destruction. Therefore, we must resist temptation immediately, even to the point of physically running away from it if we have to. If we don't, it will produce a downward spiral. It begins with the desire in our eyes and if we don't resist it, sin is birthed. Then before we realize it, we are taken captive. All of this can happen in the blink of an eye! This is because our flesh is weak.

Matthew 26:41:

> Watch and pray that you may not enter into temptation. The spirit indeed is willing, but the flesh is weak."

Good news! There is a way out as described in 1 Corinthians 10:13:

> No temptation has overtaken you that is not common to man. God is faithful, and he will not let you be tempted beyond your ability, but with the temptation he will also provide the way of escape, that you may be able to endure it.

How do we resist temptation? Pray and resist! Our flesh is weak and in order to overcome it, God must help us. We can't do this on our own! He provides a way out for us; we just have to go to Him and be willing to take the exit He provides.

1. What temptations do you struggle with?

2. Has God helped you overcome a particular temptation? Explain.

You are *loved.*
You are *worth it.*

Notes

We are **surrounded** by so many lies.

It is time to start *fighting* with the **truth.**